Twelve
Baskets
Full

CHRISTIAN FOCUS PUBLICATIONS

© 1992 Christian Focus Publications
ISBN 1 85792 008 2

Published by
Christian Focus Publications Ltd
Geanies House, Fearn, Ross-shire,
IV20 1TW, Scotland, Great Britain.

Cover design
by
Creative Link,
Edinburgh

Scripture references are mainly from the
New International Version,
published by Hodder & Stoughton,
and the King James Version.

Printed and bound by
The Cromwell Press, Broughton Gifford, Melksham

JANUARY

ELIZABETH CATHERWOOD

Faith In God

Faith
Hebrews 11

For many, New Year is a time for parties and for singing Auld Lang Syne. But for other people, the start of the year can bring thoughts of anxiety and even sadness. We look back and remember those who are no longer with us, and we look forward and wonder what lies ahead of us.

Furthermore, we live in times when to be uncertain is almost regarded as a virtue. 'Honest doubt' we are assured is a good thing and we are told by everybody - even some Church leaders - to question everything and never to say that we are sure of anything.

Now no one would disagree more strongly with that attitude than the author of Hebrews. The Christians to whom he wrote were full of doubts - about Jesus Christ, about the way of salvation and about their own beliefs. So the whole letter is written to encourage them; he wants them to have 'full assurance', and, in the great eleventh chapter, he urges them above all to have the faith which will make them confident and secure, whatever may happen to them.

And the source of this confidence? 'Jesus Christ is the same yesterday and today and for ever' (Heb. 13:8).

JANUARY 1

Sure And Certain
Hebrews 11:1

In chapter 10:38, the writer has quoted the prophet Habakkuk, who said, 'But my righteous one will live by faith. And if he shrinks back, I will not be pleased with him.' 'But,' the wavering Hebrew readers are assured, 'we are not of those who shrink back and are destroyed, but of those who believe and are saved.'

The trouble with many of us - as with those early Jewish Christians - is that having believed in Christ for salvation, we often become despondent, because we cannot see any outward proof of the blessings of our belief. Like the psalmist in Psalm 73, we see the unbelieving people around us flourishing, while we struggle and find things difficult. But this, says the writer, is what faith is all about. We know that we have 'Christ in us, the hope of glory,' and it is our faith that makes us absolutely sure of that, even at times when the glory we hope for is veiled in the mists of the trials and perplexities of life. At such times we cannot see clearly, but our faith in God, and in his promises, makes us certain. 'We live,' as Paul says in 2 Corinthians 5:7, 'by faith, not by sight.'

JANUARY 2

TheAncients
Hebrews 11:2

What troubled the Hebrews was that, having become Christians, they had begun to suffer. They had, we read in Chapter 10:33, been 'publicly exposed to insult and persecution'. They had been put in prison and had had their property confiscated, and at first they had accepted this joyfully. They had 'stood their ground' but now they had begun to lose their confidence. They were looking back to their old Jewish ceremonial practices, and the writer has taken much time to remind them that all these were just a picture of what was to come - the once-for-all sacrifice of himself by the great High Priest, Jesus Christ.

But he wants to show them, too, that the highly-venerated heroes of their history - 'the ancients' - were also sharers with them in God's way of salvation. He has told them in Chapter 3:3 that 'Jesus has been found worthy of greater honour' even than Moses, their great law-giver; and now he wants to make it abundantly clear that all the heroes of the past were saved, not by their sacrifices and offerings, nor by their deeds, but by their faith. It is this, he says, for which they were commended.

The Universe
Hebrews 11:3

Since the early 19th century, nothing has been used more aggressively in an attempt to undermine the Christian faith than the whole question of the origin of the universe. The theories of evolution are put forward with increasing dogmatism until people forget that they are, after all, only ideas which can themselves be overturned as a new piece of information comes to light. The general tendency has been to set scientists against Christianity, and to regard as naive those who believe that God created the universe as we read in Genesis 1.

But, according to the author of Hebrews, it is an essential part of our faith to believe that God was the creator. Furthermore, he shows that our faith enables us to 'understand' the creation: that 'the universe was formed at God's command' and that he brought it all into being from nothing. So we must not be intimidated by science. Rather, by faith, like the godly scientists of the 17th century, as we study the book of God's word, so we must study the universe, 'the book of God's works,' and accept and rejoice in what we find there.

JANUARY 4

Abel
Hebrews 11:4

Having laid down some principles concerning faith, the writer now turns to illustrations of this from Old Testament history. He starts almost as far back as he can, with Abel, Adam's second son, who died so tragically by his brother's hand.

Yet it is not his murder but his faith that the writer wants them to remember - the faith which enabled him to understand God's will so well that he brought a sacrifice which was acceptable to him while Cain's was not. Commentators vary in their explanation of why this was so, for Genesis simply says that God looked with favour on Abel and his offering. But this verse in Hebrews makes it clear that Abel's heart was right before God - 'it was because of his faith, expressed by what he gave, that he was reckoned righteous' (Alan Stibbs).

Furthermore, we are reminded that though he died long ago in the days of earliest history, his faithful desire to please God still has much to teach us. Also we must never forget that there is only one sacrifice that is acceptable to God, that of his Son; and it is only through him that, like Abel, we find favour.

JANUARY 5

Enoch
Hebrews 11:5a

We read of Enoch five times in the Bible: in Genesis 5, where he appears in the list of the fathers before the flood; in the genealogies in 1 Chronicles 1 and in Luke 3; then in this verse; and finally in a remarkable little passage in Jude 14 and 15. His life on earth was much shorter than that of the other men in the Genesis genealogy and its end was clearly supernatural. Genesis said that 'God took him away', while Hebrews underlines this by saying that 'he did not experience death' and 'could not be found'.

He was a prophet too, as we see in Jude, with an understanding of the holiness of God and his coming judgement upon sinners. But what we learn above all about Enoch is the closeness of his relationship with God. He 'walked with God' is the wonderful way in which Genesis describes this. It was by faith that he pleased God. And so when God took him early from this world, it was as the old Puritan writer described: 'He changed his place but not his company, for he still walked with God, as in earth, so in heaven.'

May that be our prayer for ourselves too.

Pleasing God
Hebrews 11:5b,6

We have seen in past days that faith is that which makes us unshakeably certain of those things which we hope for but cannot yet see; and this is illustrated in many ways throughout the chapter. But in verse 6 we learn another vital truth about faith: we see it, as it were, from God's side. The writer makes a solemn pronouncement: 'Without faith it is impossible to please God,' and then he goes on to explain why he has used this strong and exclusive word.

We need to be absolutely sure first of all that God exists, and that he alone is God (not a vague multiplicity of spirits as we so often hear in our pluralistic religious society). Furthermore, we must realise that he is not some remote being, but a loving personal Father who always responds to and blesses - 'rewards' - those who seek him. But we must not turn to him in a detached, academic sort of way. We must earnestly seek him; like Enoch, we must walk with him and learn of him if we are to know his blessings in Christ. And faith is God's way for us to come to him.

Noah
Hebrews 11:7

The writer now moves on to Enoch's great grandson, Noah, a man who also 'walked with God'. He lived in terrible times - 'wicked', 'evil', 'corrupt' and 'violent' are the words used in Genesis to describe them, yet, in spite of it all, he maintained his fellowship with God. So God revealed to him that he would destroy all life on the earth, but also that, in mercy, he would spare Noah, his family, and representatives of all living creatures, in an ark which Noah should build.

Noah's response was threefold. He believed what God had told him; he obeyed him implicitly; and he 'preached righteousness' (2 Peter 2:5) to others and warned them of the coming judgement. He did all this in spite of the carelessness and mockery of other people, because 'in holy fear' he was certain of what he could not see, and he knew he would be saved because his hope was sure. And we, too, heirs with Noah of the righteousness that comes by faith, must tell the unbelieving world of a more final judgement than the flood and of a salvation in Christ far more wonderful than the ark.

JANUARY 8

Abraham - The Land
Hebrews 11:8-10

'We are Abraham's descendants,' the Jews once said to Jesus, and this was their great source of pride. So when he writes to his Jewish readers about Abraham, the author deals more fully with him than with anyone else; not only because of his historical greatness but because he was, as has been said, 'Faith's exemplar *par excellence.*'

The first illustration of this is the way in which, obeying God's call, he left his home and country and, not knowing where he was going, set out for the country which God would give him. Even when he arrived there, he did not possess it - apart from a burial plot - but had to live in tents. And he did all this 'by faith'. He believed God about the promised land, but even more, he saw beyond that to a great eternal city - not a passing earthly one, but a heavenly one with foundations, made by God himself.

Paul tells us that we are Abraham's offspring, if by faith we turn our hearts from the world and set out on the journey to the heavenly city, believing, like Abraham, in the promises of God.

Abraham - The Son
Hebrews 11:11-12

'Against all hope, Abraham in hope believed.' That is how Paul in Romans 4:18 describes Abraham's faith concerning the birth of Isaac. He did not 'waver through unbelief', even though he was very old and Sarah was barren as well as being past child-bearing age. God had promised, and Abraham knew that he was faithful. And so, though Abraham was 'as good as dead', from him came countless descendants, believing Jews and Gentiles alike for 'he is the father of us all'.

There is much discussion amongst the commentators - even the Bible versions differ here - as to whether, in verse 11, the writer is referring to the faith of Abraham or that of Sarah - 'who laughed first in unbelief, then learned to laugh in faith' (Trapp). But both were involved in the great redeeming purpose of God through the seed of Abraham, 'meaning one person who is Christ' (Galatians 3:16). Abraham knew this. There, thousands of years before Christ came, Abraham saw the Saviour's day and was glad. And we who can look back at the cross of Christ are glad with him and praise 'the God of Abraham'.

JANUARY 10

A Better Country
Hebrews 11:13-16

'The world is too much with us', wrote the poet Wordsworth, and this is certainly true of the materialistic society in which we live. But it is often true also of Christian people. As our Lord said, 'The worries of this life, the deceitfulness of wealth and the desire for other things come in and choke the word' (Mark 4:19), and so we mentally and spiritually settle here on earth.

But this was not true of the patriarchs. Though they were the heirs of the things promised, they died without seeing their fulfilment; but they saw them by faith - though afar off - and they rejoiced at what they saw. So sure were they of the better country and city which their God was preparing for them, that they not only declared that they were strangers on earth, they also showed no desire to turn back to their old ways.

This must have struck home to the first Hebrew readers who were looking back, but what of us? Our citizenship is in heaven, so we, too, should live as aliens in a strange land, trusting fully in the Saviour, who through his death and resurrection has gone to prepare a place for us.

JANUARY 11

Abraham - The Sacrifice
Hebrews 11:17-19

These verses remind us of one of the most moving stories in the Old Testament - God's call to Abraham to sacrifice Isaac. We see how Abraham showed supreme faith: an unshakeable confidence in God, even when faced with a terrible situation. Because together with his agony at the thought of sacrificing his son must have been his bewilderment that this should happen to Isaac, who was so miraculously born and through whom God's promises were to be fulfilled.

But Abraham was 'the friend of God'. He knew from experience that God was just: 'Shall not the Judge of all the earth do right?'; all-powerful: 'Is anything too hard for the Lord?'; and faithful: for when he gave the promise, 'because he could swear by no greater, he swore by himself.' So Abraham 'reasoned' that in the fulfilment of the promise, even raising the dead was not impossible with God, and by faith he obeyed God's command. And God blessed that faith and provided the sacrifice. 'When God tries faith, it is to give still greater blessing. Let us not fail God, but as at the beginning of the life of faith, so in the trial of it, be like our father Abraham' (Wuest).

JANUARY 12

Isaac, Jacob And Joseph
Hebrews 11:20-22

Having looked in detail at the faith of Abraham, the writer comments more briefly on that of his immediate descendants, and in each case, he draws attention to the same quality in their faith. These three dying saints were sure that what they hoped for would certainly happen. They knew that God had a purpose for Abraham's seed: 'Many nations will serve you', said Isaac to Jacob, and Jacob himself spoke of God's promise to make him 'a community of peoples'; while Joseph was so sure of the promised land that he eschewed a ruler's tomb in Egypt and arranged that he was to be buried with his fathers in Canaan.

Isaac also saw that God's promises are not subject to human customs, so in spite of Jacob's deception he did not change the blessing at Esau's request. The same understanding of God's ways was then given to Jacob himself when he gave the greater blessing to Joseph's younger son. Furthermore, he was so overwhelmed on another occasion by the faithfulness of God, that, frail old man though he was, he bowed down and worshipped. In their lives these men had experienced God's goodness and in their deaths they testified to his promise.

JANUARY 13

No Ordinary Child
Hebrews 11:23

We come today to the writer's second full portrait - that of Moses. The great law-giver was another venerated figure of Jewish history, so much so that in Chapter 3 the writer has to remind his readers that Jesus is 'worthy of greater honour than Moses'. But this was not to detract from Moses' outstanding faith and here in Chapter 11 we are shown some aspects of this.

We see first the faith of Amram and Jochebed, Moses' parents, who acted with wisdom and courage in a time of severe persecution. Quite apart from their natural affection and their desire to protect him from death, the implication here is that they recognised that there was something remarkable about the child. Stephen also described him as 'fair in the sight of God' (Acts 7:20). By faith, Moses' parents hid him, in spite of the king's threats, and protected him later, so that in God's providence he was given back to them.

The Jewish Christians had been rendered fearful by persecution, as so many have been since, whatever form the persecution may take. 'Live by faith in God, as this couple did,' says the writer, 'and do not be afraid of the king's edict.'

JANUARY 14

Disgrace For Christ
Hebrews 11:24-26

So the Jewish baby became a member of the royal household 'educated in all the wisdom of the Egyptians', but when the moment of crisis arrived, Moses knew where his true loyalty lay and he did not hesitate to ally himself with the despised Hebrews. This meant leaving all his royal privileges and going into the wilderness, but he did so because his faith gave him an understanding of what the true issues were - something this epistle's first readers needed to grasp.

He realised that the Hebrews were God's people and that being one with them was far more important than enjoying the sinful pleasures of the godless. Secondly, he saw that those pleasures were but transitory, because, like the other people of faith, he was confidently 'looking ahead to his reward'. Thirdly, because of this, Moses saw that the true treasure was to suffer disgrace for Christ - 'the reproach of the coming Messiah to whom he was united by faith' (Hughes).

We do not like to be despised, but as Christ suffered for us, the writer exhorts us in Chapter 13:13 to, 'go to him, outside the camp, bearing the disgrace he bore,' looking for the city that is to come.

JANUARY 15

God Our Saviour
Hebrews 11:27-28

In their interpretation of verse 27, commentators differ as to whether the writer is referring to Moses' flight to Midian or to his leading the people out of Egypt. But whichever view we accept, the vital point of this verse is that he was not controlled by a fear of Pharaoh; rather, says the writer in a wonderful paradoxical phrase, he endured because 'he saw him who is invisible'. He looked ahead to his reward, as we saw yesterday; but more than that, he kept his gaze fixed on God himself and trusted the one who said, 'I will be with you.'

Furthermore, Moses believed God's warning about the destruction of the first-born. Therefore in implicit obedience to God's command he led the Israelites to sprinkle the lamb's blood upon their door-posts to protect themselves from 'the destroyer'. The Jewish Christians were hankering after their old ceremonial observances but the writer has already shown them in earlier chapters that these were only pictures of the atoning death of Christ the Lamb of God. Moses believed God's way of salvation and so we, by faith, accept Christ our Passover who has been sacrificed for us.

JANUARY 16

The Red Sea
Hebrews 11:29

Soon after they had kept the first Passover, the faith of God's people was tried to the limit. In one of the most dramatic Old Testament stories, we see the terrified children of Israel with mountains on either side, Pharaoh's army behind them and the sea before them. How often have Christians felt like they did then - pressed in on all sides by mountainous problems, other people against them, minds rushing about in a panic, and to all appearances no way out.

What an encouragement, therefore, for the first-century Christians, and for us also, to be reminded of Moses' call to the Israelites: 'Do not be afraid. Stand firm ... The LORD will fight for you; you need only to be still' (Exodus 14:13-14). And when God divided the Red Sea before them, by faith they passed through, awed by the display of his power and with a renewed trust in him. We, too, need to 'still and quiet' our souls, knowing that when we are tempted, God will provide a way out so that we can stand up under it (1 Corinthians 10:13).

And the Egyptians? They just 'tried to' go through, but they had no faith in the living and all-powerful God, and they perished.

JANUARY 17

The Walls Of Jericho
Hebrews 11:30

One of our troubles as Christians is that we are over-awed by the might of our adversaries. We have seen how the people of faith, trusting in the greater power of God, did not fear mighty and godless rulers. And we, in our day, have witnessed the fall of those who set themselves against God and his people. But there are other enemies, mighty bastions of intellectual, spiritual and moral unbelief that seem impregnable to the message of the Gospel.

The walls of Jericho must have seemed unconquerable to the Israelites. But with patient faith they carried out God's commands, using only the means that he had chosen, and on the seventh day, at their shout of triumph, the walls of the city fell. And when we seek to 'demolish arguments and every pretension that sets itself up against the knowledge of God', 'the weapons we fight with are not the weapons of the world. On the contrary, they have divine power to demolish strongholds' (2 Corinthians 10:5,4). We 'shout' the gospel of repentance towards God and faith in our Lord Jesus, and by faith wait to see God bring down the walls of unbelief in the hearts of men and women.

JANUARY 18

Amazing Grace
Hebrews 11:31

'Can any good thing come out of Nazareth?' Nathaniel asked, and this scepticism can often be true of us also. We tend to assume that God can only work in certain ways and through certain people, and the first readers of this epistle may well have taken for granted that faith could only be demonstrated by virtuous members of Israel. But here, standing with Abraham and Moses, the writer puts Rahab - a Gentile, a woman and a prostitute.

Her faith shows the saving work of God in that, as with Lydia in Philippi, he opened her heart so that she believed in the God of whom she had heard. Not only that; she believed it with great certainty. 'I know,' she said, 'that the Lord has given you this land' (Joshua 2:9). Thirdly, as James points out, she demonstrated her faith by her obedience. Risking her own safety, she protected the spies, because she was sure that the God of Israel would save her and her family.

And so, the honour of being in the genealogy of Jesus Christ was given to one who had been a prostitute. Let us never be high-minded; we are all sinners, saved by grace.

JANUARY 19

Difficult Days
Hebrews 11:32

Like many a preacher, the writer finds that his time is running out. So he now has to limit himself simply to mention some further outstanding people and achievements of faith. The first four to which he refers lived in the time of the Judges, a time of lawlessness when 'everyone did as he saw fit.' But even in those days, there were men and women who, however hesitatingly and erringly, believed in God and obeyed his commands. Two such men were Barak and Jephthah. The former refused to go into battle unless Deborah went too, and the latter marred his victory by the tragic rashness of his vow, but they 'conquered kingdoms' and 'routed foreign armies' by their faith.

The late twentieth century seems to mirror the time of the Judges in many ways. Moral and spiritual anarchy is all around us and people reckon that all that matters is what they themselves want to believe and do. We are told in Judges 11:29 that 'the Spirit of the Lord came upon Jephthah'; and we must pray that he will come upon us also, so that the unbelieving Canaanites and Ammonites of our day will fall before his truth.

JANUARY 20

Gideon
Hebrews 11:32

We have been thinking over the past days about some of the great men of our Christian heritage. They were people of such towering faith that their example can both daunt us and inspire us.

Today, however, we see a very different character, Gideon, whose faith was so weak that he constantly needed to be bolstered up and encouraged. He was so unsure that God was calling him to lead his people that he asked him for a very specific sign - that a fleece should be wet while the ground around it was dry. And then when God graciously answered that prayer, Gideon, just to check that everything was all right, asked God to repeat the miracle, but the other way round!

He was anxiously aware of his own insignificance, 'insecure' as people would say nowadays, and yet here he is among the great ones. Perhaps he is of particular encouragement to many of us who are as uncertain as he was, because we see in his story the infinite patience of God with his weakest people. And we see too that God can use even us in his service as 'mighty warriors' in his strength.

JANUARY 21

Samson
Hebrews 11:32

Samson's story must be one of the most tragic and yet one of the grandest in the Old Testament. God gave him an extraordinary gift which was to be used in the service of his people. It was a gift that carried with it the need to obey certain specific commandments, and for many years Samson used his great strength to lead God's people and to conquer their enemies. But then he allowed his own uncontrolled desires to take over; he treated God's gift lightly and he and the Israelites were overcome by the Philistines.

But Samson in his blindness and bitter captivity turned back to God in prayer. 'O Sovereign LORD,' he said, 'remember me. O God, please strengthen me just once more...' (Judges 16:28). And the wonderful part of the story is that God heard him and answered him. In fact he used him more in his death than he had ever used him in his life. We also may, like Samson, go far from God, but we need not despair. If we come back to him and ask his mercy, he will accept us and use us again for his glory.

David
Hebrews 11:32

We could wish that the writer had had time to develop the story of David and his faith. His life and his psalms have been a constant source of encouragement and comfort to God's people, and in him we can see faith in many aspects. He had a passionate sense of the greatness of God and a desire that he should be honoured. 'Who is this uncircumcised Philistine,' he said of Goliath, 'that he should defy the armies of the living God?' and it was this motivation that made him 'powerful in battle'. His whole life was controlled by it: 'I have set the Lord always before me,' he wrote; and when he sinned, his agony was that he had dishonoured God.

Secondly, he knew that God cared for him and had a plan for him, and even in the dark days when he did not understand what was happening to him, his faith enabled him to trust in the Lord's deliverance.

Thirdly, through his faith, he saw the Messiah, his 'greater son'. He knew that God would not let his 'Holy One see decay' and that through him, we shall 'dwell in the house of the Lord for ever.'

Samuel And The Prophets
Hebrews 11:32

Much of the Old Testament is taken up with the words of the prophets, those men who stood before the people and taught them the ways of the Lord. Samuel guided the people from the rule of the judges to that of the kings, and at the end of his life called the people to witness that he had faithfully 'administered justice'. He and all the prophets exhorted the people to live lives of faith and obedience - 'If you do not stand firm in your faith,' said Isaiah, 'you will not stand at all' (Isaiah 7:9).

The prophets often did this in the face of acute suffering, but 'the word of the Lord' consumed them - 'his word is in my heart like a burning fire,' cried Jeremiah - and their faith in him empowered them. We live in the days when the prophetic voice is rare. Truth itself is in question, the Bible is regarded as an interesting religious document and people use their own opinions as the final criterion. Let us pray that God will give us prophetic leaders who will bring us back to the authority of the Word of God, whose cry will not be, 'I think', but 'thus says the Lord'.

Facing The Lions
Hebrews 11:33

The writer must have been thinking supremely of Daniel here, the majestic man of faith who strides through the reigns of the Babylonian and Medo-Persian kings. Throughout his life, in the most dangerous circumstances, he relied unwaveringly upon the faithfulness of God and the truth of his word. He had no fear of kings and rulers. He was a great man of prayer, and when towards the end of his life he was faced with death if he continued to worship God, he did not hesitate but openly prayed as usual. And when the punishment was carried out, 'no wound was found in him, because he had trusted in his God,' the God who had 'shut the mouths of the lions'.

We in our day need more men and women of faith in positions of leadership. Life is not easy at the top - rulers can still be as capricious as Nebuchadnezzar or Darius. But instead of condemning politics as a dirty game, we should support and pray for more leaders like Daniel, who will maintain the faith and influence their colleagues, so that like Nebuchadnezzar they may say, 'Surely your God is the God of gods and the Lord of kings.'

JANUARY 25

The Fiery Furnace

Hebrews 11:34

The story of Shadrach, Meshach and Abednego is one of the most dramatic stories in the Bible. Children love it because of its crescendo of excitement, and Christians are stirred as they read of the fourth figure that was with the men in the furnace. Sometimes, because we know the end of the story, we fail to consider the faith of the three friends who, knowing the result of their decision, refused to worship Nebuchadnezzar's statue. However, it is this faith, which 'quenched the fury of the flames', that the writer commends to his first-century readers who might be facing similar fiery trials.

Like the earlier heroes, the three were not overawed by the greatness of the king; they knew that the God whom they served had the power to deliver them even from the fire. But also - and this is still more remarkable - even if he did not do that, their faith in him and their loyalty to his service was such that they would never worship another, come what may. But God did deliver them. The arrogant king was humbled and Christians of all times have drawn encouragement from their story.

JANUARY 26

The Shunammite Woman

Hebrews 11:35a

'Women received back their dead, raised to life again.' He does not mention them by name, but the writer must have been thinking here of the widow of Zarephath and the Shunammite woman. The latter is a remarkable example of faith. She is described as a 'great' woman but she was also a spiritual woman, who recognised that Elisha was a true prophet of God. So she both offered him regular hospitality and gave him a permanent room of his own.

God rewarded her with a child, but when the terrible day came that the boy suddenly died, it was then above all that she demonstrated her faith. She realised that her only hope was Elisha; she would not be deflected by anyone else, but went straight to the prophet, poured out her grief to him and refused to leave him until he himself did something about it. Someone said of her, 'She could not take her child to the prophet, so she begged the prophet to go to her child' and this is what we, too, must do. We must ask the Lord himself to deal with those whom we love, because, ultimately, it is he alone who can help them.

JANUARY 27

Even Unto Death
Hebrews 11:35b-38

Most of the stories which we have been considering over the past weeks have shown faith triumphantly delivering men and women from all manner of trials. Now in these verses, the writer turns to those whose triumph of faith was even in death itself, and he is probably thinking here not only of Old Testament people but also of the terrible persecution of faithful Jews by Antiochus in the time of the Maccabees.

The horrifying list in these verses of the sufferings of God's people can be repeated throughout Church history. We think, for example, of the Christians in the Roman arenas; the tragic deaths at the time of the Reformation; the Covenanters in Scotland; the days of the Boxer rebellion in China and more recent stories of persecuted Christians in many countries.

And often, as we think of these things, we feel that were we in similar circumstances we would never stand as they did. But they were people like us. It was their faith in the faithfulness of God and their steadfast hope in what was before them that, through the Holy Spirit's power, kept them faithful unto death. And God will keep us too.

JANUARY 28

Made Perfect Together
Hebrews 11:39-40

The amazing thing about the faith of all the people in this chapter is that they exercised it so steadfastly without having received the promise. We know that they saw it 'afar off' and that they were travelling towards the heavenly city, but it was God's plan that both they and we should be 'made perfect' together. And so, though it is we who have been given the indescribable blessing of seeing the fulfilment of the promises in Jesus Christ, yet 'the household of God consists of the faithful participants of the Old Covenant and the members of the New' (Brown).

We still need to live by faith, because the final consummation of the promises is yet to come, and if our privilege is great, so is our responsibility. Calvin puts it perfectly: 'If those on whom the great light of grace had not yet shone showed such surpassing constancy in bearing their ills, what effect ought the full glory of the gospel to have on us? A tiny spark of light led them to heaven, but now that the Sun of righteousness shines on us, what excuse shall we offer, if we still cling to the earth?'

JANUARY 29

The Witnesses
Hebrews 12:1

One of our greatest blessings as children of God is that he has not left us to struggle on alone, but has put us into his family so that we may receive from our brothers and sisters all the encouragement and comfort that we need. The Christian life is not easy and the writer compares it to a long and hard race that we must run with patience and determination, deliberately getting rid of everything that would hinder us from sticking to the course. But there in the grandstands all around us, as it were, are thousands upon thousands - a 'cloud' he calls them - of God's people from the past, cheering us on and witnessing to the faithfulness of God.

'Do not turn back and be discouraged,' the writer tells his first readers. 'I have been telling you about some of those witnesses. They ran the race and they finished the course, so be encouraged by their example and press on.' We need this exhortation too. Thank God for the faithful men and women throughout the history of the Church whose lives move us and inspire us to continue in faith to the end.

JANUARY 30

Consider Him
Hebrews 12:2-3

We saw yesterday how the writer urges us to look at past believers in order that we may be strengthened to persevere in our faith. But now, in these verses, he gives us the greatest encouragement of all - Jesus, the Saviour who has made everything possible. 'Fix your eyes on him,' he tells us, and the form of the verb he uses implies that we must always keep on doing so. It is through Jesus that our faith began and he is the one who will perfect it. He can sympathise with us, because as the Pioneer of our salvation he was made perfect through suffering, and it is as we consider him who was obedient unto death for us that we shall not 'grow weary and lose heart'.

And he endured it all, the cross, the shame and the opposition because of 'the joy set before him'; that fullness of joy in the glory of his Father's presence, which he has promised that we shall share with him to all eternity. 'To me to live is Christ,' says Paul, 'and to die is gain,' so let us run our race in the days ahead, always looking to him who is both the goal and the prize.

FEBRUARY

PHYLLIS THOMPSON

The God Who Guides

I Will Guide Thee

Psalm 32:8

The primary secret of obtaining guidance from God is faith in him, confidence that as we place our lives in his hands he will take control, and will not leave us to wander alone. The Lord Jesus assured his disciples that like a good shepherd he would call his own sheep by name and lead them (John 10:3). David asserted, 'Commit thy way unto the LORD; trust also in him; and he shall bring it to pass' (Psalm 37:5). Solomon reiterated the importance of faith when he wrote, 'Trust in the LORD with all thine heart, and lean not unto thine own understanding. In all thy ways acknowledge him, and he shall direct thy paths' (Proverbs 3:5-6).

The apostle Paul affirms that for those who are in Christ Jesus there are 'good works which God hath before ordained that we should walk in them' (Ephesians 2:10). Time and time again in the Bible we have such reassurances. 'He will be our guide even unto death' (Psalm 48:14). He can be trusted to guide us right to the end of our mortal life.

'My Lord knows the way through the wilderness,
All I have to do is to follow.'

Scattered... Preaching
Acts 8:4

'Many Christians know little or nothing about personal guidance from God. They go from event to event and live a kind of hand-to-mouth spiritual existence - a spiritual and moral opportunism. They have no sense of working out a plan of life under God's guidance. They have little or no sense of destiny or mission.' So wrote Dr E Stanley Jones years ago, his worldwide ministry giving him a unique opportunity to observe the spirit of the age.

How different were the believers in the early church, who recognised, in the very persecution they were suffering, the means used to uproot them from their security that the gospel might be spread abroad! Scattered from Jerusalem we find them preaching wherever they went. Through these un-named believers the church in Antioch was formed (Acts 11:19-21), the church that will always be remembered for at least two reasons. It was here that the name *Christian* was coined (Acts 11:26), and it was in this church that the Holy Spirit singled out Paul and Barnabas, to set the pattern for missionary enterprise. They were sent out, not only by the Holy Spirit, but also by the church (Acts 13:1-4).

The Carnal Mind... Enmity

Romans 8:7

Mankind is fundamentally rebellious. This is the crux of our difficulties in walking with God, the cause of guilty fears which we cannot always define.

It was so in the case of the young woman who had already learned something about the forgiveness and peace that comes after humble confession of sins. But she was still vaguely conscious that there was more to experience, and she went on praying and seeking, expecting an increase of peace and joy. To her dismay she realised that the opposite was happening. She was oppressed with the feeling that something was wrong, and she did not know what it was.

At last, on her knees one evening, came the terrifying realisation that in her heart she hated God. She could not alter this, she must confess it - but to tell God she hated him! She wondered if she would be blasted out of existence.

Instead, she had a revelation. She saw a leering old man - her self. And she saw Christ on the cross. Then she realised that when he died there, he took on himself her old nature and bore the punishment. After that she understood the words in Romans 6:6: 'Knowing this, that our old man is crucified with him...'

FEBRUARY 3

When Ye Pray, Believe...
Mark 11:24

In our anxious search for a deepening of our spiritual lives, we are apt to look for dramatic experiences, a conscious empowering. No doubt there are times when such things happen, but in some cases God works in a different way, quietly and imperceptibly, as in the episode in 2 Kings 3, when three armies were without water, and the word of the Lord came, 'Ye shall not see wind, neither shall ye see rain; yet that valley shall be filled with water...' and it happened.

An earnest young Christian had been praying fervently for the Holy Spirit's power in her service, and was waiting for some manifestation in herself; but none came. One day, going off to lead a children's meeting, she picked up a book on the hall table, and opened it at random. Her eyes fell on the words, 'What things soever ye desire when ye pray, believe that ye receive them, and ye shall have them.' So she knelt down and prayed for the Holy Spirit's empowering - believing. Then she went off to the meeting. For days her faith fluctuated. Then it dawned on her that although she had no exultant feelings herself, there was a spiritual awakening among the children! It had happened!

FEBRUARY 4

To Thy Holy Habitation
Exodus 15:13

We tend to think of guidance only in connection with our daily lives, our outward activities, and especially our service for God. But another sort of guidance is needed in what might be termed 'the journeyings of the heart'. The guidance of God is all bound up in his ultimate purpose for us - to bring us to his holy habitation, to fellowship with himself. The ardent desire of the apostle Paul was to know Christ Jesus his Lord (Philippians 3:8). Jesus himself said, 'This is life eternal, that they might know thee the only true God, and Jesus Christ whom thou hast sent' (John 17:3).

This personal knowledge of God demands holiness. 'Without holiness no man shall see the Lord' (Hebrews 12:14). And although, like justification, it is imparted through faith, the inworking of it, like sanctification, is a deepening experience, and usually a painful one. The trials of Job were greater than most of us could bear, and although they eventually led to far greater blessing in every way, that blessing did not come until Job cried, 'I abhor myself, and repent in dust and ashes.' I abhor myself...

FEBRUARY 5

Paths Not Known
Isaiah 42:16

'I will lead them in paths that they have not known; I will make darkness light before them, and crooked things straight.'

It was certainly true in the experience of the young medical student whose sights were set on going to China. She was apparently in perfectly good health when she applied to the missionary society in which she hoped to serve, and it came as a shock when, after her medical examination, she was told she had tuberculosis. Did this mean she could never go to China?

Two years of treatment passed before she was pronounced clear of the disease and could apply again. But during that period she had learned all the latest methods of treating tuberculosis. When she eventually arrived at her destination in China, she knew the reason for the delay. There was a high incidence of tuberculosis in the area, and she was now well qualified to treat the sufferers who came to the Mission hospital. In the years that followed, a string of people emerged from the hospital - healed of tuberculosis by the doctor who herself had once contracted it.

FEBRUARY 6

Bread Corn Is Bruised
Isaiah 28:28

Dimly conscious of our spiritual superficiality we sometimes pray, 'Dig deeper channels, Lord,' then wonder why we are led in strangely bewildering and painful paths.

A Christian, who had been working for several years in a remote rural area, had been praying earnestly for someone she knew who was working among prostitutes in a great city. When the exigencies of war forced her to that very city, she found that the one she had been praying for was herself praying for a fellow worker. Everything seemed to point to her being the right one, and joyfully she went forward.

Then the confirming sign for which she had prayed was rather dramatically withheld. Then doors began to close. Eventually, the only one that opened was back to that remote rural area... Over the months that followed she learned the truth of the words: 'There is a peace that cometh after sorrow; of hope surrendered, not of hope fulfilled... 'Tis not the peace that over Eden brooded, but that which triumphed in Gethsemane.'

FEBRUARY 7

If We Confess...
1 John 1:9

The young woman had had a clear-cut conversion. Having once lived for pleasure, dancing, gambling and cinema-going, she now devoted herself to Bible study, prayer, visitation and children's work. Then she went to a conference where the emphasis was on the Holy Spirit, who gives power for service and Christian living, though many Christians do not realise this, and go on working in their own strength. One of the speakers said that he had been doing that for ten years before he started seeking the Holy Spirit.

'Ten years! After a few months I am seeking the Holy Spirit... I must be making good progress spiritually!' she found herself thinking. Then came the thought: 'But that's spiritual pride! And spiritual pride is sin.'

Her mind was in a turmoil. She tried to argue herself out of her self-satisfaction, the feeling of her own superiority, but in vain. Pride! At last, wearied with all she had heard, she remembered 1 John 1:9. In desperation she prayed, 'Oh God, I'm proud. I confess this sin of pride.' She could do no more, fight no more, think about it no more.

A short time later she realised, to her amazement, that the pride had gone!

FEBRUARY 8

Held In With Bridle
Psalm 32:9

Horses and mules need bit and bridle to keep them in the right way, and sometimes God's servants find themselves brought up with a jerk.

A Christian worker who had lived uncomplainingly enough in an uncongenial neighbourhood, on retirement grasped at circumstances that gave her the opportunity to get away. She let her house, and started looking around for somewhere pleasant, praying, of course, that the Lord would guide her. But she began to feel in a spiritual fog. At her request, relatives were looking out for something in her own home town, but without success, and one of them observed, quite casually, 'Perhaps it's the Lord's will for you to go back to your house.'

The words cut like a surgeon's knife, revealing the true condition within. 'That's just what I don't want!' she exclaimed. But the words 'Go back!' rang in her mind with an authority that she recognised, as a horse recognises the pull of the bridle. So she went back, realising that the conditions of discipleship had not changed - 'if any man will come after me, let him deny himself...'

The neighbourhood did not become more congenial, nor the conditions of living easier, but the spiritual fog lifted.

FEBRUARY 9

Commanding The Ravens
1 Kings 17:4

God uses a variety of means to lead and encourage his people.

From the point of view of the American missionary couple stranded in England, the provision of their fare back to the USA was all part of their walk with God, and they thanked him as well as the human donor, for surely he had guided her to give it.

They did not know what it had cost her. God had guided her through her Bible readings to give them the money - it was what she had saved up to go home to Malaysia on a longed-for holiday. Not without a pang had she relinquished her own home-going.

If no one else knew, God knew. What prompted one of the patients she had been nursing to give her some money? How did it happen that someone inadvertently dropped a bank-note on the very pavement she passed along a short time later? Finally, why did her brother, in the same period, give her some odds and ends of gold he had collected, and now decided he did not want? She was able to sell them for a good price; and so, one way and another, she received the money she needed for her own fare home.

Lending To The Lord
Proverbs 19:17

Faith grows as it is practised, and it is often practised in secret, before it becomes obvious. God starts guiding his people early. David's famous victory over Goliath had been preceded by lonely encounters with a lion and a bear (1 Samuel 17:34-36).

Hudson Taylor's name became famous in his day as the founder of a 'faith' mission (China Inland Mission) but as a young medical student he was led into a situation which left him penniless. He had gone into a dangerous slum area at the request of a man who pleaded with him to come and pray for his dying wife. On arrival he found a starving family. In his pocket was his last coin. He needed it badly himself, but the need of this family was greater than his, so he gave it to the poor father. He remembered, 'He that hath pity on the poor, lendeth to the LORD.' He must trust God.

Next morning, while eating the last of his porridge, the postman arrived. A small packet addressed to him from an anonymous donor contained a pair of kid gloves - and a coin worth four times the amount of what he had given away.

God is no man's debtor!

FEBRUARY 11

Call Unto Me...
Jeremiah 33:3

The Chinese pastor was at his wits' end. He was treasurer of a little indigenous missionary society reaching out to the remotest borders of his country, and he was suddenly presented with a bill he could not possibly pay. The man to whom the money was owing must be paid the following day. Two hundred silver dollars! Where was that coming from? All he could do was to pray.

Thousands of miles away in England a business-man began to feel uneasy. He had written to his daughter in China, telling her he would be sending her some money for the little Chinese society she had told him about, and had planned to send it by the usual channels, which took two or three weeks. But the uneasiness persisted. He must send that money *now*. So he cabled it - involving an intermediary in Shanghai in an unwelcome midnight call to receive and forward it. The money reached his daughter early in the morning, and she passed it on to the pastor immediately. It was two hundred silver dollars.

Show Me A Sign
Judges 6:17

When the Lord suddenly calls an apparently ordinary, uninfluential person to a task for which he feels utterly inadequate, it is not surprising if he shrinks from it, fearful of proceeding without some reassuring confirmation.

The story of Gideon has been an encouragement to many, for when the angel of the Lord appeared to him and told him he was to save Israel from the Midianites, he asked for such a sign; and God granted it, not once, but three times. The first time fire came up from the rock and burned up the flesh and unleavened bread Gideon had placed there. The second time the fleece Gideon placed on the floor became wringing wet, as he had asked, while all around was dry.

Gideon was still not completely convinced, though his own lack of faith made him uneasy. 'Don't be angry with me, but please prove once more that it is you,' he said in effect, and asked that this time the fleece should be dry, and the ground all around wet. 'And God did so that night' (Judges 6:40).

The exercise of faith at that early stage strengthened Gideon for the apparently impossible campaign in which, with only 300 men, he routed the enemy.

FEBRUARY 13

Thine Own Understanding

Proverbs 3:5

Preconceived ideas, formed from the purest of motives, are not necessarily the right ones.

The man who was looking through the *Situations Vacant* in the paper, passed over the announcement that a well-known Christian publishing firm was looking for a marketing manager, without giving it a thought. He had been born and brought up in Christian surroundings, and believed he ought to be witnessing for Christ in the secular world, where he already had a job, marketing furniture.

But God had a different plan. The visit of a little family highlighted that Christian publishing firm again, as one of the children drew attention to its Handbook on a shelf. ('Uncle Tony's book', she called it, though he had merely had a hand in producing it.) But not until a day or two later when, looking through the *Daily Telegraph*, he again saw that Christian publishing firm's advertisement for a marketing manager, did he stop and consider.

He decided to apply for the job, trusting God to open or close the door. He was promptly accepted. And that is how he found his true vocation, in the Christian publishing world.

FEBRUARY 14

Not Forsaking Assembling
Hebrews 10:25

The exhortation 'not to forsake the assembling of ourselves together' is one that we do well to observe, for it is not only a safeguard against drifting, it also provides moral support and spiritual enrichment.

Wherever he went in his own country, the young Christian student always sought out a Christian gathering, to which he could attach himself. But when he arrived in England for study he contented himself with praying privately and reading his Bible. This he did regularly, but he was not really happy. He was wondering about marriage. Was it God's will that he should remain single? He got to the point where he was willing even for that. But he was very lonely.

Then one day he met someone who invited him to come along to a gathering of Christian students - from his own country! Very gladly he went, and found himself completely at home with them. His whole life was enriched, and he realised what he had been missing through not seeking Christian fellowship. He did not make the mistake again; he went regularly to church and fellowship meetings after that. And it was here that he found that God had prepared for him what he earnestly desired - a godly wife.

FEBRUARY 15

Prove Me Now...
Malachi 3:10

There are times when it is genuinely difficult to know what is the right course to take - to remain prayerfully and patiently in a situation where things seem to be going wrong, or to get out.

Scriptures can be found to support either action, and a young missionary home on furlough was feeling the need for a clear directive from God. Something had happened on the field over which a colleague had resigned, and she wondered if she ought to do the same. So she prayed specifically that if she should return to her field of service she would have the money to pay for her own fare.

Early in her furlough she earned a little money, sent it to the mission towards her fare - and forgot about it. The months passed; the time was drawing near for her return when suddenly she received a gift which nearly covered the fare - *but not quite*. Did this mean that she should resign? She was in a dilemma, and went uneasily to sleep. Next morning she was awakened by a memory. The money she had already paid in and forgotten was the exact sum needed to pay the full fare! All doubt was removed - she went back.

I, Being In The Way
Genesis 24:27

This is not only the story of the bringing together of a man and a woman for the fulfilling of God's purposes, but also of a faithful servant through whom it was brought about. Abraham's servant had been sent by his master to find a wife for his son Isaac. He was told to go to Abraham's kindred to find her, and Abraham assured him that the Lord would send his angel before him. Arriving at the place, he wondered how he was to know the one whom God had appointed. So he prayed specifically. His prayer was for a young woman who was healthy enough, and warm-hearted enough, to draw water for ten thirsty camels. Then Rebekah came to the well, and offered to do just that!

The answer to his urgent prayer assured him that he was on the right track. And it provided him with a suitable argument when he reached Rebekah's home, and asked for her hand for his master's son, Isaac.

'This is from the Lord,' said her father and brother. Even more assuring than the gold and silver the servant produced as evidence of Abraham's wealth was that answer to prayer.

FEBRUARY 17

Wilt Thou Go?
Genesis 24:58

When the healthy, high-spirited daughter of Bethuel, Rebekah, awoke that fateful morning, there is no reason to believe that she realised she had come to the turning point in her life. She probably had a daily routine, like most people, and to go to the well to draw water was part of it. And it was no unusual thing, on arriving, to see a rather weary traveller with ten camels resting there. Nor was it unusual to be asked for a drink.

But what prompted her to draw enough water to quench the thirst of ten camels? She had not heard the stranger's prayer. Yet it was that impulsive, warm-hearted act which amazed him - and decided her own future.

'Thou knowest not what a day may bring forth.' The revelation that the stranger had come from her uncle Abraham, of whom she had heard but certainly had never seen, was followed by the news that he wanted a wife for his son and by her own unselfconscious act she had proved to be the one God had appointed. Yet it remained for her to acquiesce.

'Wilt thou go?' she was asked. Her heart had been prepared. 'I will go,' she said.

The Lord God Brought Her To The Man

Genesis 2:22

In the beginning of time God created woman as a help-meet for man, and it was God who brought Eve to Adam. How many times since then he has done the same thing!

When the young missionary about to sail for China saw a beautiful girl sitting in the front row of the farewell meeting, he felt strangely drawn towards her, though he did not even know her name. He was glad when he saw her indicate her desire to follow the Lord by standing at the preacher's appeal, but it was not until three years later that he even saw her photograph. It was in the magazine of his own missionary society, as one of the new workers.

Then he heard that she had been designated to the very province in which he was working. 'When Rebekah comes on the horizon "thine ears shall hear a word behind thee" - and there will be no doubt in either your mind or hers,' wrote a wise friend to whom he had written asking about marriage.

He met her at last when there was a gathering of the missionaries, and, as his friend prophesied, there was no doubt in either of their minds. They were engaged within a month.

FEBRUARY 19

I Shall Arise...
Micah 7:8

The stops in life are usually difficult to accept or understand, especially when we seem to be travelling in the right direction.

The sixteen-year-old girl, a young Christian, had set her heart on going to the Watch Night Service, and the sense of disappointment when her parents refused to allow her to be out alone so late at night was very deep. Disappointment, Discouragement, Doubt... The Deadly Ds threatened to bring her down. She went to her room, and, miserably opening her Bible at random, read,

'Rejoice not against me, O mine enemy: when I fall, I shall arise; when I sit in darkness, the LORD shall be a light unto me.'

It became her text for life. She trained as a nurse, but an arthritic back put an end to nursing. The stop led to a different path, doing clerical work in the nursing world, and this time it seemed to be for good. But she was forced to retire on grounds of ill health. However, recovering gradually, her former skills proved useful as she found openings for lecturing. In her seventies she was still on platforms - speaking at women's meetings!

FEBRUARY 20

Acknowledge Him...

Proverbs 3:6

God has various ways of guiding people, and in the case of the man who was thinking about moving because his wife had a bad heart, God spoke through a sermon. It was a very practical sermon, in which the preacher pointed out the sort of mistakes people make - one of which was putting their job before their church. 'Job; buy new house; sell old house; then look for a church.' That is the wrong order, he said. 'Better to start finding the right church, selling the old house before buying the new one, and then taking a job within reach,' was the advice he gave, thus putting God first. One member in his congregation, at least, decided to follow that pattern.

He knew the church he wanted to be associated with, for the vicar and his wife had already inspired him spiritually. He sold his house, then looked for something in their neighbourhood - and found a bungalow. No stairs for his wife to climb! And he soon found just the right job, within easy reach of church and home.

'In all thy ways acknowledge him, and he shall direct thy paths' he had often read in Proverbs 3:6, and he had found it to be true.

FEBRUARY 21

Counsel Of The Lord
Proverbs 19:21

There are occasions when a course of action has been under discussion, but a final decision put off - and a higher Power takes over. A childless couple who longed for children were told of a brother and sister suitable for adoption, so they went along to see them. The children were asleep, only their black curly hair visible over the bedclothes. The couple returned home in pensive mood. The husband was not sure he wanted dark-skinned children in a white-skinned family. 'Does it matter?' said his wife. They were still undecided when suddenly the telephone rang. It was a call from the orphanage, asking if they wanted to make an appointment.

The moment of decision had come. If they did not intend to go ahead, they must say so now. There was no opportunity for discussion. They looked at each other silently - and knew what they must do. They made the appointment. 'The counsel of the Lord, that shall stand.' When they saw the merry-faced little boy, and the little girl who asked, 'Are you going to put your arm round me?' they knew they had been guided aright.

FEBRUARY 22

He Leadeth Me...

Psalm 23:2

In a fallen world hurt, pain and suffering are inevitable. No amount of care or self-protection can prevent it. 'Man is born to trouble as the sparks fly upward,' wrote the wise man.

But God works with patience and wisdom to bring healing in unexpected ways, as the Australian nurse found after she arrived in England. There had been traumas in her childhood that she wanted to forget, and she had not found her niche in her own country. In England she had got on better, but then her health broke down and she was in a dilemma. She could not stand the strain of hospital life, so what was she to do?

The Christian leader to whom she went for advice told her of a home for retired missionaries, where they needed a nurse on the staff. She applied, and was accepted. Travelling to her destination, to her surprise the words 'I will pour you out a blessing' flooded her mind. She was not expecting a blessing - only a job! But God's promise was fulfilled. The matron of the home became like a mother to her, providing just the relationship she had been lacking. She was lonely no more.

FEBRUARY 23

The Lord That Healeth
Exodus 15:26

The parents-in-law of the young divorcee could understand her bitterness. She had been wronged by their son, and they did all they could to help her, praying very earnestly for her as she moved to a new and strange district. It proved to be the first step in the course of events that led to her inner healing.

The vicar called to welcome her to his parish, and discovered that her father-in-law was one whom he had heard preaching years before. It provided a point of contact, and she started going to church occasionally. Then she decided the children ought to be baptised, and what impressed her was the solemnity of her own vows. She felt she must take 'religion' seriously, and went to church more regularly.

When an evangelistic mission was held in the village she went with her children to the morning meetings, not wanting to leave them alone in the house at night. At those meetings for children, she herself met the Saviour; and as his life flowed into her heart, the bitterness was flushed out. Peace was restored, and it was peace on a sound basis - a love that would never change, the love of one who would never betray her.

FEBRUARY 24

Two Sides Of A Coin
Proverbs 18:17

The Book of Proverbs contains many wise precepts, and one verse in it settled the mind of a middle-aged man who, only a couple of years before he was due for retirement, changed his job.

He had done his best as a policeman, but had come to the point where he felt he could put nothing more into his work. While expediency indicated it would be sensible to stick it out and draw a full retirement pension, he decided that rather than fossilise he would look for another job. He saw that a firm of Christian solicitors were advertising for a managing clerk, and phoned for an application form. He was invited to go immediately for an interview - and was offered the job.

One misgiving remained. As a policeman he had often had to give evidence against apparent law-breakers. Now he might be called on to defend the very people he had helped to prosecute. Was it honest to do this? Then he read the reassuring words in Proverbs 18:17: 'He that is first in his own cause seemeth just; but his neighbour cometh and searcheth him.' That settled it. Prosecution and advocacy were merely two sides of the same coin.

FEBRUARY 25

I Have Chosen You
John 15:16

While it is heart-warming to be conscious of being chosen by the Lord for a certain task, there are times when it can be very disconcerting, especially when one is established in one's present work and the new call is to something for which one feels entirely inadequate.

A nurse, working in a very remote area where she was obviously needed, reacted strongly against the letter that came to her, asking if she was willing for her name to be put forward to become principal of a training college in her own country. In her reply she pointed out all the reasons why she would not be suitable, ending by assuring the committee of prayer that they would find the right person. Privately she asked God that if he wanted her, the committee would be *unanimous* in inviting her. It seemed unlikely!

Some weeks later three letters arrived by the same post. One was from the chairman inviting her, at the unanimous request of the committee, to accept the post. The second letter confirmed it. The third was from a friend telling her, 'You are the woman for the job.' God's choice was confirmed.

FEBRUARY 26

The Spirit's Restraint
Acts 16:6-7

How can we understand the withholding of the Holy Spirit when everything seems to point to a certain course of action? Paul and Silas must have been mystified when on their missionary journey they were unexpectedly restrained from going to certain places. And the restraint was not from any outward circumstances. They were 'forbidden by the Holy Ghost' in one case, and in the other 'the Spirit suffered them not'. Something inward stopped them from going to either place, so they moved on and eventually the place of God's appointment was revealed.

The same Holy Spirit restrains in these days, in individual lives, as the young man who had worked in insurance for six years discovered when he was told he would be made redundant at the end of the year. He was offered another job, but had no conviction that it was in God's plan for him. Something inward restrained him, and he refused it. After that he heard that the manager of the local Christian bookshop was leaving at the end of the year. Then his own church elders asked him to take it on. He had no experience in such work; the salary was lower - but it proved to be God's place for him.

FEBRUARY 27

An Angel Before Thee
Genesis 24:7

When the Lord leads his servants in unexpected paths, he often gives them a signal ahead of time, some indication that a change is coming. They do well to heed it.

An elderly woman who had sold her home to go to live with a friend thought she would spend the rest of her life there. It came as a surprise when the words 'Ye have dwelt long enough in this mount' (Deuteronomy 1:6) came to her with a significance that she recognised. Experience had taught her that when the time came, she would understand; and sure enough, a few months later, her friend died.

She had the option of remaining on in the house, and it would have been the reasonable thing for her to do. But those words from Deuteronomy were the signpost indicating she should move out, and she obeyed. Then it emerged that most of the legacies would have remained unpaid had she not done so, for until the house was sold the capital was insufficient to fulfil all the bequests. And the sheltered accommodation into which she moved proved much more suitable than the house she had relinquished!

FEBRUARY 28

MARCH

R. T. KENDALL

The God Of
The Second Look

God Keeps His Own
Jonah 1:1-2

I identify with Jonah; I know what it is to have the word of the Lord come to me 'a second time'. You see, Jonah is a type of the Christian life. There is not one of us, I hope, who has not known the chastening of the Lord; because if we do not know it, we are not Christians (Hebrews 12:6).

We are all Jonahs. We know what it is to be thrown overboard and swallowed up until finally we surrender and admit that God's way is right. What a great doctrinal truth underlies this book! Some call it 'the perseverance of the saints', while others call it 'eternal security', but the truth which Jonah illustrates is that God keeps his own.

I also love this book because it shows in many ways how God converts a sinner. How many of us went the opposite way when we first heard his word? How many of us have even experienced the severity of God's wrath in our rejection of him? God has a way of getting his way and it may be painful for us. But we will learn that 'salvation comes from the Lord'.

God's Unexpected Plan
Jonah 1:2-3a

God may ask us to do something, and it does not make sense to us. God may have a plan for us, and we are trying to figure out the end from the beginning. Why would God say to Jonah, 'Go to Nineveh'? And God may be directing us in a certain way we don't understand. It may be the thing that God is asking us to do. We say, 'I can't do it. It's too big for me. I am afraid. Besides, I can't understand why God would say, "Do that".' But who would have thought that God had any plan for Nineveh?

We don't even know whom God is going to convert next. Who would have thought at one time in the early church that the next person to be saved was Saul of Tarsus?

Listen, if God can save us he can save anybody. When Jonah ran away from the Lord, that might have been the end. And when we also have disobeyed, that could have been the end of us. God was not obligated to keep on dealing with us. And thankfully that was not the end of the story of Jonah.

MARCH 2

The 'Providence' Of Sin
Jonah 1:3-4a

Jonah felt confirmation in his disobedience. This always happens. Jonah determined to go to Tarshish and he found a ship going to Tarshish! He, no doubt, convinced himself that he was right.

You see, when we are living in disobedience to God's commandment, we will find many providences to confirm us in that disobedience. I have talked to businessmen who say, 'I must be doing something right. Look how God has blessed my business.' But God blesses atheists as well! Ah yes, sin can be very 'providential'. The way of disobedience has a way of providing confirmations, and the problem with the modern church is that she finds confirmation for the thing she wants to believe and convinces herself in her folly.

Jonah momentarily convinced himself he was doing the right thing.

Thank God for the happy words: 'But the LORD sent out a great wind into the sea' (Jonah 1:4 AV). 'But Jonah .... But the Lord'. How kind he is despite our determination to go in the opposite direction! Thank God we cannot run from him (Psalm 139:8). He is omnipresent. God has a way of following us (Psalm 23:6).

'But Jonah...But the Lord'.

MARCH 3

The Sleeping Backslider
Jonah 1:4-6

Had you realised that we are not aware that we were asleep until we wake up? Sometimes we relax and say, 'I am just going to rest; I am not going to sleep'. Then we realise we have slept for an hour. And this is the condition of the church - not aware of its state; not aware that it is asleep. When we are asleep, we dream of doing things we would never do if we were awake. And the church is asleep today, doing things that it does not do when it is awake. We don't like the sound of an alarm. We want to sleep on. And no one likes the alarm of the prophet. This is why Israel killed its prophets.

It finally turned out that the mariners had to wake up Jonah. I wonder whether the world will be the source of our awakening? Is that what it is going to take?

God didn't have to send the storm. He could have finished off Jonah. Thank God for the storm, and for those whom he uses. It is a sign that God is doing great things to get to us.

MARCH 4

The Providence Of God
Jonah 1:7-9

We can hurt our own testimony as Christians by not living like good Christians, making everybody around us miserable. We may be blaming them when the trouble lies with ourselves.

And so it was with Jonah on the boat. There was trouble. The sea was causing the boat to rock, and they said, 'What is causing it?' The answer was to be found right there: the problem was the man on the boat. The confusion was traceable to Jonah, and not only to Jonah but also to an angry God who sent the wind. God was at the root of all the trouble.

God overruled the mariners' confusion and superstition and they saw the real cause of the difficulty. They cast lots and the lot fell upon Jonah.

The thing to be seen at this point is that it was out of their hands. They would try anything; they were given over to chance. The lot fell on Jonah, but that was not because of anything they did; God overruled and they saw that Jonah was responsible. The real solution to the problem lay outside themselves.

MARCH 5

The Honour Of God
Jonah 1:9-10

Jonah received no glory from this awakening. It's a humbling thought.

What took place on the boat was in spite of Jonah. The mariners certainly saw nothing particularly good and virtuous in him. In fact, they were moved when they saw he was a disobedient man. But they saw behind this, that there was a real God out there. A God who was in control!

We need to reassess our prayers. We should pray for an awakening, for revival, for blessing. But we must ask ourselves whether in fact we are wanting God's glory or our own. 'I am the LORD; that is my name! I will not give my glory to another' (Isaiah 42:8). But when God comes, he will come in such a way that no one may boast before him (1 Corinthians 1:29).

The interesting thing to notice in this story is the respect the mariners had for Jonah. Now he did not deserve this respect, but they were afraid of him! And so it is that when there is a real awakening in the world, we shall see a resurrection of the respect for the church, a respect that ought always to have been there.

MARCH 6

Surprising Conversions
Jonah 1:11-16

God has a purpose in any continuing storm. None of us like stormy weather. If we are in turmoil, we may wonder, 'Why does God let this last?' We are involved in a matter that is beyond us and we wonder why God doesn't come to our rescue. 'Surely God can handle this matter?' we keep saying. *But God has a purpose in the continuing storm.*

Now in this context it was a two-fold purpose. First, God had more to teach Jonah. But, secondly, God wanted to convert the mariners.

We find these men, these heathen, becoming beggars before God, and finally dignifying the will of God. They said, 'O LORD, please do not let us die ... for killing an innocent man, *for you, O LORD, have done as you pleased.*'

There is still more. The mariners saw the need of atonement - outside themselves. We are told that the men greatly feared the Lord and offered a sacrifice to Yahweh. The mariners then 'made vows'. And notice the order. They made their vows after making the sacrifice - after atonement. You see, sanctification is our gratitude. It is a way of saying 'thank you'.

MARCH 7

At The End Of Our Tether
Jonah 1:17

Jonah expected to die. Jonah was not looking for a great fish to swallow him up!

Jonah was willing to die because he had recovered the principle that he was not his own. God has a way of bringing us back to the fundamental point of our conversion. When we were first converted we lost our lives (Mark 8:35). Jonah began to get possessive over his own life. God had to show him a lesson. May he bring us back to the fundamental point where we recognise what we were when we were first converted! We must continually be in a state of willingness to lose our lives.

When we get too possessive of something we are in danger of losing it. But when we really have lost our life, that is when we save it.

We may get too possessive about our job or our future, our husband, our wife or our children; God has a way of reminding us that he is God - and who we are.

God is never too late, never too early; but always just on time.

So it was. Jonah expected to die. But God prepared a fish.

MARCH 8

Enforced Learning
Jonah 1:17 - 2:1

We must be clear that the reason that the storm continued was not because God didn't love Jonah. The continuing storm does not mean that God is trying to get even with us.

Many Christians live under a kind of Old Testament covenant. They say, when something goes wrong, 'God's mad at me. He is getting even.' Rubbish! 'He does not treat us as our sins deserve or repay us according to our iniquities' (Psalm 103:10). If God did deal with us according to our sins we would be chastened all the time! Chastening is not God's 'getting even'. God 'got even' at the cross! God was satisfied with his Son on the cross (Isaiah 53:6).

Why does God continue to chasten? Why the continuing storm? God's chastening is not meted out in proportion to our sins but in proportion to the lesson we have to learn. The greater the work ahead, the greater the trial now. Jonah had some lessons to learn.

Thus, the fish! The chastening may seem to be more than we can bear, but God is telling us via the chastening that he has not finished with us yet. He has more for us to do.

MARCH 9

God's Strange School
Jonah 2:1-3

God has strange ways of teaching us. Jonah was learning this lesson in the belly of the fish. If we don't learn from Scripture, we will learn the hard way through God's painful chastening. What form will the belly of the fish take for us? It could be financial reverse, failure, illness, emotional problems, a rocky marriage. It could be exposing our folly before men, or withholding vindication from us.

Chastening is inevitable if we are Christians (Hebrews 12:6). It is a sign of God's love. It is also a feeling of his wrath. This is why we need to understand chastening as simultaneous wrath and mercy. Chastening is painful, and there are degrees of chastening. Furthermore, chastening is not meted out in proportion to our sin, as we have seen, but in proportion to the work God has for us to do. It is God's way of preparing us.

The Lord had prepared a great fish to swallow up Jonah. You may be in the belly of the fish but I promise you it will end (Psalm 30:5; Psalm 103:9).

The belly of the fish is not a happy place to live but it's a good place to learn.

MARCH 10

Enforced Praying

Jonah 2:4

We have emphasised that the Lord had 'prepared' a great fish to swallow up Jonah. The same Lord who prepared the fish was preparing Jonah. God does not delight in chastening; he delights in *us*. St Augustine put it like this: God loves everybody as if there were no one else to love. He goes to great pains to bring us to the place where we will conform to his will. God loves us as though there were no one else to love.

The three cardinal rules (see Hebrews 12:6-11) with regard to chastening are:

1   Chastening is inevitable if we are Christians.

2   Chastening is painful.

3   Chastening is preparation: 'God disciplines us for our good, that we may share in his holiness.'

'From inside the fish Jonah prayed...' Why not before? Because he was out of the habit of praying. Disobedience often leads to a prayerless life. Do you know what it is to be out of the habit of praying? I find praying the most difficult enterprise in the Christian life. It is hard work. And if we get out of the habit of praying it is very difficult to start again.

MARCH 11

A Cry Of Distress
Jonah 2:5-6

Jonah not only prayed; it was a cry of distress (Jonah 2:2). There is praying and then there is *praying*, and we are told that Jonah called for help.

When is the last time you wept in prayer? There is an interesting insight to be had from the story of Hezekiah in Isaiah, chapter 38. It is the account of when Isaiah the prophet came to Hezekiah and said, 'Put your house in order, because you are going to die; you will not recover.' Then Hezekiah turned his face to the wall, and prayed to the Lord. But the word came to Isaiah again, and said, 'Go and tell Hezekiah, "This is what the LORD, the God of your father David, says: I have heard your prayer and seen your tears".'

We may not have the things we want because we have not wanted them enough to cry, to weep. Are we too proud to cry? God has a way of making us cry. The interesting thing about this passage in the book of Isaiah is that tears apparently moved the heart of God. Imagine that! Thank God - he sees the tears! And they touch him.

Jonah's cry touched God.

MARCH 12

Do You Want Answered Prayer?

Jonah 2:7

Thank God for answered prayer. 'Weeping may remain for a night, but rejoicing comes in the morning' (Psalm 30:5).

I wonder sometimes if we really want God to answer our prayers. I have been counselling people in vestries now for over thirty years. I have learned that most people don't want their problems solved; they want them understood. So many of us are spiritual neurotics who thrive on affliction. We become acquainted with the way we are and don't want to change. But Jonah was forced to face his problem directly.

So, do we want our prayer to be answered? Or are we just enjoying being in the belly of the fish? Three days and three nights in Jonah's case. How long will it be in ours? Do we want to stay there? Are we happy nurturing our own neurosis, our own weakness? Do we want to be out of the fish?

Jonah said, 'When my life was ebbing away, I remembered you, LORD.' It took the trauma of praying from the fish's belly to make Jonah face his need to see God act - now. Do we really want our problem *solved*?

MARCH 13

The Folly Of Disobedience
Jonah 2:8-9

Most of us are like Jonah. Jonah is an example of one who had to learn the hard way. I want us to see today some of the lessons Jonah learned in the belly of the fish.

First, he learned that those who live in disobedience do not magnify God's mercy; they rather dishonour it (Jonah 2:8). Secondly, God wants our gratitude even though we are not saved by it (Jonah 2:9). And thirdly, he learned that salvation, in any case, was out of his hands (Jonah 2:9b).

Be careful. It is no sign of God's mercy that we get away with flagrant disobedience. There is always someone who says, 'Well, sin is sin, and we all sin; and since we are going to sin I might as well pick a good one.' Let me tell you something. Some sins are more serious than others. Any sin that affects God's witness in the world provokes his anger!

God has chosen us in Christ from the foundation of the world 'to be holy and blameless in his sight' (Ephesians 1:4). God is serious about this matter of our personal holiness and obedience.

Jonah's conclusion regarding his disobedience: it wasn't worth it.

MARCH 14

Resigned To God's Will
Jonah 2:10

God could have taught Jonah some lessons and still let him die in the belly of the fish. There have undoubtedly been those who learned lessons but did not live to tell anyone what they had learned - God took them.

Jonah learned great truths, without any promise that he would live to tell what he had learned.

At the beginning of the story Jonah ran away from the Lord. But God had worked on Jonah until he was so willing that he had become willing not to be used. Only God can turn our affections and make us want to do what we thought we never would do.

Do we know what it is like to see something clearly, something that is viable and worthwhile, and not be able to express it? Perhaps we are not articulate and we can't; perhaps we do not have the platform necessary in order to get our point across; perhaps we don't have the credentials the world expects, and so we are not going to be taken seriously; or perhaps our time has not come. We must be willing not to be used.

But God spoke; and the fish ejected Jonah!

MARCH 15

The God Of The Second Look
Jonah 3:1-2

We come now to the high watermark of the book of Jonah.

'Then the word of the LORD came to Jonah *a second time.*'

It should give us all great comfort to realise that the best of God's servants have made foolish mistakes, yet were used again. It gives me no small comfort to realise that there have been those before me who have failed to do as they ought to have done. Yet God did not hold a grudge.

God is not obligated to anyone. As far as Jonah is concerned, God did not even have to send the wind. But he did. He did not have to prepare the fish. But he did. He did not have to eject Jonah from that fish. But he did.

And he certainly did not have to come to Jonah the second time. But he did.

God doesn't hold grudges against his own.

When God comes a second time it seems none too soon. But it is always soon enough. We may feel guilty that we wasted so much time. We ask, Why didn't God come sooner? But when he comes the second time, it is soon enough.

MARCH 16

God's Unchanging Mandate
Jonah 3:2a

We are in the second half of the book of Jonah. In many ways this is the more interesting half. I might say that the second half of Jonah is also more painful for us because it exposes the motives of the human heart in even sharper focus. While the first half of Jonah shows us how God chastens his own and how he keeps his own, the second half of Jonah shows how carnal we can be, even after we see clearly what God is doing in and through us. It is appalling that Jonah, having seen the glory of the Lord, could still be so carnal. We sometimes like to think that when we have moved up a little closer to the Lord this rids us of all our maladies.

When God comes in great power, there is always the reappearance of the truths he used before. And although he may come in a slightly different way each time, there is this common denominator that brings us back to the very simplicity of the gospel.

The orders which God gives to the church remain the same. When God says 'Go', he means it!

MARCH 17

God's Unchanging Method
Jonah 3:2b

Not only are God's orders the same - 'Go to Nineveh' - but so is the method: preaching. We might wish there was another way God would save men. Paul says that 'in the wisdom of God the world through its wisdom did not know him' (I Corinthians 1:21). God has decreed that men are to be saved by preaching. Sometimes it is foolish preaching. But that is not what he really wants. He works through the foolishness of preaching. But God can even use foolish preaching.

We may be thinking, 'I am glad about that; I like good preaching. I will just come and hear preaching.' But we cannot get away with that. Preaching is something we are to do. Preaching is every Christian's business. Have we led a soul to Jesus in the past six months? Or in the past year? Or even in the past five years? When we say, 'I witness by my life', I grant that God can use that as a testimony. But when we say that, I fear it is an excuse. We ought to be so equipped that we are able to talk to anybody.

MARCH 18

God's Unchanging Message
Jonah 3:2c

The only kind of preaching God owns is *that which he gives*. Thus the message to Jonah the second time was: 'Go to Nineveh, and proclaim to it the message I give you.' So many of us have been intimidated by the spirit of the age. We seem to be afraid to let some sophisticated person know that we actually believe the Bible.

The book of Jonah tells us more about God than about Jonah. We see God in his anger, God in his tenderness. We have seen the God who hides himself; the God who shows his face; the God who controls nature; who answers prayer; who uses evil in such a way that we are tempted to justify it - as in the case of the mariners' conversion. We have also seen how God gets his way and goes to great pains to accomplish his purpose.

Have we been suppressing what the Holy Spirit has made clear he wants us to say? I cannot imagine a more miserable situation than consciously to be out of God's will.

When we are in disobedience God's Word becomes blurred. When we come to ourselves the same old message emerges clearly.

MARCH 19

A Gracious Warning
Jonah 3:3b-5

So we come to the message itself. What kind of preaching would this be? The message is summarised in eight words: 'Forty more days and Nineveh will be overturned.'

Yet in Jonah 3:5 we read these words: 'The Ninevites believed God.' We do not read that they believed Jonah - it had not occurred to them that it was Jonah's theory. They believed God.

We may think, 'Where is the love of God in this message?'

I answer: This message is bubbling over with God's love and mercy. Why? God never talks like that when there is no hope. Whenever God gives a warning in this life, that is the best sign of all!

Why did God go to such pains to give his message to Nineveh? The very fact that he should send a prophet to talk like that meant there was hope. When God's anger is visible in the world it is a happy sign.

It was a sign of mercy when God took note of Nineveh's wickedness. The way we should pray is to ask that God will discover the sin of our country. For if he discovers it - thank God! There is no warning in hell.

MARCH 20

The Surprising Revival
Jonah 3:6-7

Now we see the moment for which Jonah was being prepared . God stayed with Jonah until he was obedient.

And what happened? The people of Nineveh believed! And when God brings us through fiery trials it is not merely to make us more pious for our own sake, or to make us more godly. There is a work for us to do, and chastening is always preparation for something else - to be of service.

Jonah was not at all surprised that the Ninevites believed. His surprise was that God passed over them and did not punish them, so he pouted about that.

Moreover, the people of Nineveh were not really surprised at the message, because there is implanted in every heart the knowledge of God. Everyone has a conscience on which is stamped the knowledge of a holy and just God.

'The Ninevites believed God. They declared a fast, and all of them, from the greatest to the least, put on sackcloth.'

We are the Jonahs in the world. The church, the salt of the earth, must begin to influence the people. And so, when the people are moved, the leaders will take notice.

MARCH 21

Learning From An Unlikely Teacher
Jonah 3:8-9

We come to the most difficult part of the book of Jonah. It is verse 9, the words of the king of Nineveh. Does God change his mind?

We know that God cannot lie (Hebrews 6:18, Titus 1:2). Yet we find in this chapter - 'Forty more days, and Nineveh *will* be overturned' (Jonah 3:4). There was no 'if' clause.

Does God change his mind? There are verses that say he doesn't; for example, Numbers 23:19. But we have difficulty with a verse like Genesis 6:6, or with the story told in II Kings 20:1-6.

Does God change his mind? The problem is that we tend to approach this question with our minds already made up. We are rather like the one who said, 'My mind is made up; don't confuse me with the facts.'

We need to become empty before the Lord. If only we could be open, because we don't know. God's ways are higher than our ways. We think a certain way and expect God to come down and fit into our mould. The secret is to be found not by adopting one view and getting proof-texts to support it, but by becoming empty. That is what the king of Nineveh did.

MARCH 22

Letting God Be God
Jonah 3:10a

Yesterday's question was, Does God change his mind? The king of Nineveh followed the very principle that we ought to follow! A heathen king in this case had the right attitude; and may we Christians today sit at his feet. He said: 'Who knows?' He did not know.

The king of Nineveh received Jonah's message and made a decree reflecting unfeigned piety. He asked all to pray, to call urgently on God. He also asked men to quit their sinning. But he had this hope: 'Who knows? God may yet relent.' The king was not a theologian. Sometimes God can use a non-theological mind when theologians or theologically-minded Christians are so arrogant that he cannot break through to them.

Who knows? Do we know? Are we so sophisticated that we know in advance what God is going to do? So often we only think with one closed dimension in our outlook.

God is not meant to be fully understood. He is meant to be worshipped. When we cease to wonder, we cease to worship. 'To whom, then, will you compare God? What image will you compare him to?' (Isaiah 40:18).

Who can tell what God will do?

MARCH 23

The Obedience God Honours
Jonah 3:10

We are wise, as we have seen, to adopt the position of the king of Nineveh who said, 'Who knows?' God seeks those who ask the question, 'Who knows if he will change his mind?' He doesn't seek those who know it all.

There are two theological questions raised in this section. We have dealt with the first: Does God change his mind? The second is: Does God reward works? We can move closer to an answer to this latter question. God 'saw' what they did. The same God, mind you, who saw their wickedness. He saw what they did and this was because he chose to do so, in the same way that he chose to see their wickedness. 'They declared a fast, and all of them, from the greatest to the least, put on sackcloth.' So God affirmed the work he had done in them! This is the way God has always done it.

So it is that we who are in Christ find God's affirmation again and again. God blesses our obedience, he blesses our self-discipline, he blesses those who pray, he blesses those who study, he blesses those who give. And consequently God affirms his own work in us.

The Crooked Stick
Jonah 4:1

Most of us have feelings of inferiority, and we tend to think that others do not have the problems we have. Most of us, when we become acquainted with our own weaknesses and maladies, assume that other Christians are not plagued with the same problems.

We often think, 'If I could only experience unmistakably the power of the Lord in my life, that would surely solve my problem.' We tend to have the idea that other people have seen the glory of the Lord in a way we have not, and therefore they are free of the problems we have.

Here follows the most astonishing part of the Book of Jonah. We see sin at its worst. We examine one who had been miraculously preserved in the belly of the fish, one who had all you and I could ever dream of having as far as an intimate, undoubted experience with God is concerned. Jonah had such a marvellous revelation of God's mercy and grace to him that, humanly speaking, we might expect he would never have a serious problem again. But, alas, Jonah was still essentially the same man.

God can use a crooked stick to draw a straight line.

MARCH 25

The Jonah Complex
Jonah 4:2a

Now came the unexpected for Jonah. The Ninevites turned from their evil ways, and God 'had compassion and did not bring upon them the destruction he had threatened.' Surely anybody should be thrilled to see God move in such an extraordinary way and show wonderful mercy to people.

But here comes the unthinkable. It displeased Jonah. Jonah's reaction was completely irrational and it shows just how profound sin is in the human heart. Jonah could not rejoice; he was angry. But he prayed! Not as he prayed in the fish's belly, mind you!

I call it 'the Jonah complex', that is, self-pity, when we should be rejoicing over others being blessed.

Most of us know what it is to have 'the Jonah complex'. This account can be of comfort to us; we see that God can use men who are still frail. It shows also how one may still have problems, even after seeing God work. Never think, then, just because we experience God's blessing that we are 'set'. We need to think realistically along these lines lest we have a wrong or romantic view of what it would be like if God were to bless in an extraordinary way.

MARCH 26

The Pain Of Honesty
Jonah 4:2

Jonah took the work of God too personally and himself too seriously. He forgot that it was God's work. In fact, Jonah was so obsessed with his own reputation as a prophet that he wanted personal vindication of his prophecy more than he wanted to see Nineveh spared. He had laid himself on the line. He had a message; he preached it. The people believed God. They proclaimed a fast. God passed over Nineveh after all. But now there was an embarrassed prophet who had preached a sermon - 'Forty more days and Nineveh will be overturned.' Full stop.

Jonah wanted to go to the edge of the city and watch Nineveh burn. And he would be able to say, 'Yes, I told you so.' It did not surprise Jonah that Nineveh believed. It surprised Jonah that God did what he did.

And yet it did not surprise him. 'I knew that you are gracious.' And this is where we come further into the 'Jonah complex'. This is how we see that Jonah was without excuse. For he knew some things that were too painful for him. He brushed these aside. He repressed what he knew: God forgives others too.

MARCH 27

Clear Thinking
Jonah 4:2-3

Let's look at Jonah's knowledge of God: Jonah's 'Body of Divinity', his 'Systematic Theology'. 'I knew that you are a gracious and compassionate God, slow to anger and abounding in love, a God who relents from sending calamity.' There was nothing wrong with Jonah's theology but there was a lot wrong with Jonah. Jonah's theology was sound, but his deductions were not. And so he was in effect saying here to God, 'You have done this. You have forgiven the Ninevites. You could have done it in the first place *without me*.' Wrong.

Unsanctified logic always reasons this way. We must remember that Christianity is not a philosophy. Christianity is revelation. It is not anti-rational, it is not irrational; it is *supra*-rational; it is above reason. Jonah's anger led him to muddled thinking. Humility leads to clear thinking. Jonah's confusion, then, was applying natural reason to revealed knowledge, so his muddle can be traced to pride. He then used worldly wisdom to embellish God's Word.

How many of us examine our own conclusions - things that we have assumed to be true because we concluded them uncritically long ago? Christianity ought to teach a person how to think.

MARCH 28

The Compassionate Counsellor
Jonah 4:4-6

Now we watch God, the master psychologist, deal with his client.

There are perhaps three ways of counselling people. One approach, when we see somebody overcome with hostility, is the existential method. Sometimes it is called indirect counselling, or non-directive therapy. A person may or may not see any guilt in what he has done, and the therapist says, 'Get it out of your system; you *are* right to be angry.' Thus the person goes on his way and feels justified. Another approach is to say, 'You are *wrong* to be angry.' That is the legalistic approach, moralising, making the person feel guilty. Some people want to be told they are wrong; they enjoy feeling more guilty.

There is a third way; a free translation of Jonah 4:4 from the Hebrew is: 'You are very angry, aren't you?' Perhaps the best way a parent can react when the child is angry is: 'You're angry, aren't you?' This shows you understand. God does not condone or condemn; he understands. The wisdom from above is 'first of all pure; then peace-loving, considerate, submissive, full of mercy and good fruit, impartial and sincere' (James 3:17). That is the way God dealt with Jonah.

MARCH 29

Fragile Comfort
Jonah 4:7-9

Jonah was 'very happy about the vine'; God intended it to bring comfort to him.

But the vine was not intended to be the ultimate proof that God was with him.

Sometimes, as a temporary means of comfort, God allows us to reflect upon what he has done in us. It is the mature Christian who realises it is not the ultimate ground of comfort; it is subsidiary; only a temporary measure which God gives in our waiting for the real ground to be seen and to be stood upon.

What is our vine? Maybe it is an extraordinary answer to prayer. Or perhaps we have been given special grace with some temptation or trial. Maybe the fruits of the Spirit seem to flow endlessly out of our life and we are very happy. Our Christian life is at a peak.

God sends a worm and the vine withers. We wake up and say, 'What happened? I had a clear mind. I could feel God's presence. But he has left me.' God does not intend that 'experimental' knowledge be the permanent ground of our assurance. Because we will get too proud every time.

We must look to him alone instead.

MARCH 30

Jonah's Final Lesson
Jonah 4:10-11

We are at the end of the Book of Jonah and we may well want to ask the question, Why did Jonah himself tell this story?

The real contribution of this book is that the very revelation of God to Israel (that he is slow to anger, that he is gracious, that he is merciful) shows that mercy and grace are universal and not limited to Israel only. For Jonah said, 'I knew that you are a gracious and compassionate God, slow to anger and abounding in love, a God who relents from sending calamity.' How did Jonah know that? This goes back to Exodus 34:6.

Jonah had to learn that the very fact that God is merciful assumes universality. So God says, 'I was good to you and you did not deserve it; why shouldn't I be good to others who don't deserve it?' God puts this point in terms of a question that Jonah could not answer. And the book abruptly ends.

Did Jonah learn his lesson? I answer: he did. He wrote the book, didn't he? He became self-effacing after all. He laid himself bare. And, in telling the story, he let God have the last word.

MARCH 31

APRIL

CARINE MACKENZIE

God's Women

Elizabeth
Luke 1:57-66

Naming a new baby can sometimes cause family problems. Why was he not called after his grandfather? Why did they give her a name like that?

Elizabeth had that problem when her baby was born. Her friends and relatives were delighted for her. She had been childless for so many years, and then a baby boy was born. 'He will be called after his father Zechariah, of course,' was the general opinion of the relatives. Elizabeth spoke up. 'No. His name is John.'

This caused quite a stir. No one else in the family had that name. Elizabeth was adamant about it because the birth of this baby was a miracle. An angel had come to Zechariah, her husband, giving him the great news that Elizabeth would have a son. 'You are to give him the name John,' he was instructed.

John grew up to be a great preacher, pointing many people to the Lord Jesus Christ.

The name John means 'Jehovah has been gracious'. God has been gracious not only to Elizabeth, but to all of us in so many ways. He has showered many blessings on us every day. Do we remember to acknowledge them, realising that the Lord has done so much for us?

APRIL 1

Mary - Chosen By God
Luke 1:26-38

The people of Israel had looked for many years for the Messiah - the chosen One of God - coming to this world. The Old Testament scriptures foretold many things about his birth. It would be in the little town of Bethlehem and his mother would be a virgin.

Mary was a young Jewish woman living in Nazareth. The angel Gabriel brought startling news to her: she would be the mother of a son called Jesus, a holy child, the Son of God. Mary's first reaction was fear. 'Don't be afraid,' the angel reassured her. Mary was then puzzled. 'How will this happen,' she asked, 'since I am a virgin?' 'Nothing is impossible with God,' Gabriel explained. The power of God would come to her life in a special way. Mary's next reaction was complete submission to God's will for her life. 'I am the Lord's servant,' she said. 'May it be to me as you have said.'

What a lesson for us! Many of the providences that God sends in our lives may initially cause us to be afraid or puzzled. If we realise that God is in complete control, then we can experience that peace which passes all understanding and submit to what the Lord has planned for us.

APRIL 2

Mary - Mother Of Jesus
Luke 2:1-20

Jesus was born in humble surroundings in the town of Bethlehem. His mother had no modern facilities or comforts - not even a proper room - but the young Jesus was lovingly cared for.

An angel of God informed some shepherds of Jesus' birth. They made the journey into the town to see for themselves this momentous event. The shepherds saw the young child in the manger, Jesus the Son of God. They returned to their work glorifying and praising God and they spread the word to all they met.

Mary treasured up all these things and pondered them in her heart. So many amazing things had happened. The most wonderful of all was the birth of Jesus, the Saviour of the world, the Saviour that Mary needed too.

These amazing things have an effect on our lives as well. Do we value the provision of a Saviour? Is it something we treasure and think about often? What joy Mary must have felt in thinking about her Saviour!

What an uplift to us if we can pull our thoughts away from the daily grind to 'consider the Lord'. 'May my meditation be pleasing to him, as I rejoice in the LORD' (Psalm 104:34).

APRIL 3

Mary At The Wedding In Cana
John 2:1-11

It can be embarrassing to have unexpected guests call at the house and find that there is nothing to give them to eat. How much more embarrassing if the guests have been especially invited!

Mary was a guest at a wedding in Cana along with her son Jesus and his friends. The wedding-feast was an important part of the proceedings and to run short of anything was serious.

Mary brought the news to Jesus, 'The wine is finished. They have no more.' She realised that he could do something about it, so she told the servants, 'Do whatever he tells you.' Jesus then performed his first miracle changing the water, usually used for ceremonial washing, into the very best of wine. This was Jesus' first display of his glory and power.

Mary was confident in Jesus' ability and willingness to help in this problem. When we have a problem, no matter how mundane, we too can take that problem and simply tell it to Jesus. There is nothing that is too little to pray about. What comfort we often lose by trying to work out our problems on our own rather than casting our cares on the Lord, 'because he cares for you' (1 Peter 5:7).

APRIL 4

Anna
Luke 2:36-38

Any grandmother loves to receive the latest photo of a new baby grandchild. It is usually given pride of place in the sitting-room, or else produced from the handbag to show to any interested friends. She is delighted with the photograph but how much more delighted when the baby comes to visit. The photo is good but the baby is better!

Anna, the prophetess, was a widow, eighty-four years old. She knew from the Scriptures that God was going to send a Saviour to the world, and she spent her time worshipping, fasting and praying in the temple.

One day her dreams became reality. Mary and Joseph had taken the baby Jesus to the temple in Jerusalem, when he was eight days old, to present him to the Lord in keeping with the law. Anna, in the temple as usual , saw the Lord Jesus and recognised him as the Saviour. How thankful she was! She had been pleased with the prospect of the Saviour, just as a grandmother is pleased with a photograph, but how much greater was her joy to see the child in reality. Everyone she met heard about him.

APRIL 5

Mary Magdalene
Luke 8:1-3

Mary of Magdala was a woman who was dramatically changed by God. Her life was in a mess and Satan was in control.

One day Jesus met Mary and by his powerful word cast out the evil spirits which had been ruining her life. She became a new creature. What a change her family and neighbours would notice! Her life's work was now no longer doing the devil's business but following the Lord Jesus Christ. She spent her time listening to him as he preached. She spent her money, along with other women, supporting Jesus and his disciples. As well as giving her time and possessions, she gave her heart which was most important. She loved Jesus so much because she had been so greatly delivered.

We might think it impossible for someone possessed by seven evil spirits to be changed. But Mary Magdalene's life shows us that 'nothing is too hard for the Lord'. His saving grace is sufficient for every one of us too. He still changes lives. Each conversion is a miracle. Sinners under the power of Satan become saints with Jesus as their Master.

'Sin shall not be your master' (Romans 6:14).

Woman Of Faith
Luke 8:43-48

Friends of ours have two very impressive trees flanking the entrance to their garden. The trunks are really massive. Many years ago a horse-shoe was nailed to one of these trees but today there is absolutely no sign of it. The wood has grown year by year and now completely envelops the horse-shoe. The owner knows it is there because he put it there.

The Lord Jesus knows each one of us. He knows if there is faith in our heart, because if there is he has put it there.

One sick woman came to Jesus very nervously. She had been suffering from internal bleeding for twelve years and no doctor could help her. She came up to Jesus in a crowd of people one day. 'If I can just touch the hem of his clothes,' she thought, 'I believe I will be made better. No one need ever know.'

She did manage to touch Jesus' hem and she was healed, but Jesus knew what had happened. He knew that there was faith in her heart because he had put it there.

It is a comfort to remember that 'the Lord knows those who are his' (2 Timothy 2:19).

APRIL 7

Woman Of Samaria
John 4

The woman went to draw water at the well at noon, the hottest part of the day, when few people were around.

A Jewish man was sitting by the well resting. 'Will you give me a drink?' he asked. It was a big enough shock that he would speak to her, a Samaritan and a woman, but to ask a favour! She was not very polite to the man, reminding him of old quarrels between their races.

But the man continued to speak with her, telling her some amazing things about himself and herself. She tried to shift the conversation from her immoral life by raising the question of the religious differences between the Jews and the Samaritans. Yet the man continued to raise the important matters about her own life and her spiritual needs.

He told her plainly that he was Jesus Christ, the Son of God. She believed him and immediately went to find others from her village to tell them about this man. As a result many believed in Jesus too.

A simple trip to the well, where she met Jesus, had changed her life. We have the privilege of meeting with him every time we read the Bible. There he speaks to us time after time.

APRIL 8

Martha The Worried Housekeeper
Luke 10:40

A woman's work is never done! All housewives will agree with that. There always seem to be a hundred and one things to see to, especially if visitors are coming.

Jesus was once visiting a family in Bethany - two sisters Martha and Mary and their brother Lazarus. Martha was very anxious that everything should be in order, so she busied herself preparing food and tidying up. Meantime her sister was sitting listening to Jesus, and this so annoyed Martha that she complained to Jesus. 'Tell Mary to give me a hand. I can't be doing all the work myself.' Jesus gently rebuked Martha for being too taken up with cooking and cleaning. Other things were more important.

We can learn from Martha's mistake. She had fallen into the activity trap - doing many things, even things which are right and proper, but becoming over-anxious and bothered about them. We too can become so busy that we forget our priorities. We must learn to be more like Mary and spend longer listening to Jesus in his word, the Bible, and speaking to him in prayer.

'Your face, LORD, I will seek' (Psalm 27:8).

APRIL 9

Mary Of Bethany
Luke 10:42

Yesterday we saw how the Lord showed Martha the danger of being so distracted by earthly cares that she was neglecting her spiritual needs. Her sister Mary had a different attitude. She spent the time sitting at Jesus' feet, listening avidly to all that he said. Jesus thought that this was a more important occupation than serving the food. He commended Mary.

'Only one thing is needed,' he said. 'Mary has chosen what is better, and it will not be taken away from her.'

The only thing that was necessary for Mary is also the only thing that is necessary for us. There is nothing that is more important than listening to what the Lord Jesus has to say to us. We have his word, the Bible, readily available to us . How important to read it often or to listen to it! Verses that we have learned and stored up in our minds will stay with us always. They will prove to be a comfort in times of sorrow, will give good advice when we have a problem, and will encourage us to do good.

Let us be like Mary and be eager to hear what Jesus has to say to us.

APRIL 10

Martha And Mary Share Their Grief

John 11

When death comes to any home, what devastation and grief that causes! Where can we turn to when a loved one is taken from us?

Sorrow came to Mary and Martha's home in Bethany. Their brother Lazarus became sick and died and many people gathered at their home to try to comfort them. When Martha heard that Jesus was close by, she immediately went out to meet him. After they talked together, she confidently stated her belief in Jesus, the Son of God, who had come into the world. Then Jesus inquired after Mary, so she, too, left the house to go to meet him. His sympathy was evident to all who were standing by, and he showed his love for them by weeping with them at Lazarus' grave.

In times of distress or bereavement, we too can find comfort and help from the words of Jesus to Martha. 'I am the resurrection and the life,' he said. 'Whoever lives and believes in me will never die.'

Death is not the end. For the Christian death is the gateway to glory in heaven with the Lord, which is far better. The Lord has conquered death.

APRIL 11

The Syrophoenician Woman
Mark 7:24-30

A Greek woman from Syrian Phoenicia came to Jesus, begging him to cure her daughter who was gravely ill. The disciples wanted to send her away, and even Jesus seemed to ignore her at first, telling her that his work was to help the Jewish people.

These set-backs did not deter the woman. 'Lord, help me!' she implored. 'It is not right to take the children's bread, and toss it to their dogs,' said Jesus. Would this reply discourage her completely? Would she still persevere? 'Yes, Lord, but even the dogs under the table eat the children's crumbs,' she replied. She would be content with a crumb.

Her faith was rewarded. Jesus granted her request and cured her daughter. Perseverance in prayer is rewarded.

Have you ever seen a father hold out a clenched hand to his little one? 'I have something for you in here,' he says. The child eagerly grabs his hand and prizes open the fingers one by one to reveal the gift, perhaps a sweet. Jesus wants us to be like that child. The gift is all the more appreciated when patience and perseverance are needed. Our loving Father longs to give us every good and perfect gift.

APRIL 12

The Widow's Mite
Luke 21:1-4

The Lord Jesus wants our whole-hearted service. His love to his people is so amazing that anything less than our all is not good enough.

One day Jesus was watching people going into the temple. On the way in they put their offering of money into the collection-box. Jesus noticed some rich men throwing in large sums of money. They had plenty and they would hardly miss their contribution.

He also saw a poor widow putting in her offering - only two mites. Not very much, we would think, just a fraction of a penny. What would Jesus think of that? 'She has given more than any of the rich men,' he said. 'She is so poor but she has given everything she had.'

Jesus takes notice of what we do for him. He wants us to give, not grudgingly, but cheerfully.

Money is not the only thing and perhaps not the most important thing we have to give to Jesus. What about our time? Are we giving that ungrudgingly and cheerfully to him?

Can we say, like Frances Ridley Havergal,

> Take my moments and my days,
> let them flow in ceaseless praise.

APRIL 13

Widow Of Nain
Luke 7:11-16

How sad it is to hear of a woman who is a widow! She has known the comfort and companionship of her husband but now has to cope with life on her own. If the widow has a family, she finds them a great support and consolation. A good son will take his father's place in providing for his mother.

The woman who met Jesus in the town of Nain had great sadness. Not only was she a widow but her only son was also dead. The woman was now alone. Big crowds of people were with her at her son's funeral, but none of them could comfort her.

The Lord Jesus saw her and had pity on her. How tenderly he spoke to her! Then he came to the young man, touched the coffin and said, 'Young man, I say to you, get up!' With that word of power, life was given to the dead and the young man was given back to his mother.

How wonderful to realise that Jesus sees our needs too and has pity on us! Our need is great. Our sin causes us great misery. His powerful word alone can help us.

APRIL 14

Peter's Mother-in-law

Matthew 8:14-15

Can illness ever be a blessing? I am sure Peter's mother-in-law would say 'Yes'. She became very sick one day and had to stay in bed. A visitor came to the house that day but she could do nothing to help prepare the food.

The visitor was the Lord Jesus. He touched her hand and immediately her illness was cured. What love and thankfulness she must have felt to him! This love was transformed into action as she set about serving a meal to the Lord who had touched her life in a special way.

Judy, a missionary in the Amazon, can also say that illness is a blessing. Years of work went into learning the language of the Apurina Indians, writing it down, then translating parts of the Scripture. Later Judy became very ill with meningitis and pneumonia. Drifting in and out of consciousness, while waiting for the plane to take her to hospital, she became aware of one Indian lady kneeling beside her praying for her. This was the first outward sign that this lady had shown of an interest in God and his message.

What an encouragement to Judy in her sickness - a visit from the Lord Jesus himself!

APRIL 15

Jairus' Daughter
Mark 5:22-24 & 35-43

Every morning I go into my daughter's room and say, 'Time to get up, dear.' Sometimes the response is an unwilling groan, but usually one call is enough.

Jairus' daughter lived for twelve happy years in her home with her parents. Probably she was wakened each morning by her mother with the Aramaic words '*Talitha koum*!' which means 'Get up, little girl!'

Distress and fear came to this happy home when the little daughter became ill. Her anxious father went to find Jesus. He fell on his knees before the Lord and humbly begged him to come and heal the child.

Jesus did not immediately go to Jairus' house. He stopped to help another sick woman. Jairus must have been impatient about the delay, but Jesus was teaching him a lesson: 'My time is best.' Delay in answering prayer does not mean denial. An answer to our prayer may not be, 'No!', but, 'Wait a little!'

While her father was away the little girl died and the family and friends were devastated. But Jesus went into the girl's room with her parents, took her hand and spoke the familiar words '*Talitha koum*!' - 'Get up, little girl!' These loving words brought her back to life.

APRIL 16

Mothers Of Jerusalem
Luke 18:15-17

A mother went to see her minister one day. 'I feel the Lord is calling me to do mission work,' she said. 'How many children do you have?' he asked. 'Four,' she replied. 'Well, there is your mission field,' she was told.

What a responsibility a mother has for the children in her care, and what an opportunity! Her privilege and her duty is to bring them to Jesus from their earliest days, for no one is too young to come to the Lord.

Mothers in Jerusalem brought their children to Jesus so that he might bless them. The disciples were displeased about this and tried to send them away but Jesus called the youngsters to him. 'Let the children come to me,' he said. 'Don't try to keep them back. Those who belong to the kingdom of God are just like little children.'

John is over eighty years of age now. Recently he was telling one of his earliest memories. His mother was washing his face and said, 'Now, John, you need more than your face washed. You need Jesus to wash your heart.' Those words stayed with John and proved to be a blessing to him. What an encouragement for any mother to bring her children to Jesus!

APRIL 17

Woman With The Lost Coin
Luke 15:8-10

We recently lost a packet of slides. We scoured the house, the car, the office - with no success. They seem to have vanished into thin air. We have looked and looked but so far we have not found it. We have given up the search now.

Jesus tells a story about a woman who had lost a silver coin. She lit a lamp and swept her house thoroughly until she found it. This was a particularly difficult task in those times. The floor would have been earthen and very little light would have entered the house. What rejoicing and relief when she found her valuable possession! She called her neighbours and friends to share her good news.

'There is joy in heaven among the angels of God when one sinner repents,' Jesus told us.

When Jesus searches for a lost sinner, he never fails to find. He does not give up as we did, and when he does find he never loses. Sinners found by Jesus are safe; no one can snatch them out of God's hand.

What a comfort in difficult times to remember that Jesus has said about his people, 'I have protected them and kept them safe'!

APRIL 18

The Ten Virgins
Matthew 25:1-13

Jesus told several stories with the same message - the importance of being prepared to meet God.

One story is about ten virgins or bridesmaids who were waiting for the bridegroom to come. All the girls had lamps with them but the five wise virgins had brought oil with their lamps. So when the bridegroom arrived they were ready to go into the wedding feast. The foolish girls, who did not have enough oil with them, went off to buy some more and so missed the arrival of the bridegroom. Indeed they missed the wedding banquet altogether.

'Keep watch! Be prepared!' is the lesson that Jesus is teaching us. Each one of us will meet the Lord Jesus one day, either at death or when he returns to judge the world. How can we be ready for that day? Only by trusting in him for salvation. Believing in the Lord Jesus is the preparation that we need.

How do we know that we are truly believing?

We can ask ourselves the question, 'Is Jesus precious to me?' If the answer is 'Yes', then we do believe because 'unto you who believe he is precious', Peter tells us in his letter. What a comfort that is!

APRIL 19

The Persistent Widow
Luke 18:1-8

Have you ever had a persistent salesman at the door? Often you do not really want to buy anything, but to stop him bothering you any more you give in and make a purchase.

Jesus told a story about a persistent widow who wanted a judge to help her with a legal matter. The judge did not care at all about the woman, but eventually he gave in and agreed to take up the woman's case because he did not want to be worn out by her constant pestering. Even an unjust man can be reached by persistent asking.

God is the good, just and perfect judge. If we continue to pray earnestly and persistently, will he not hear us and take up our case? Jesus told this story to encourage us to pray always and not to give up.

God is not like the unjust judge. He wants to hear from us at any time.

> What a privilege to carry
> Everything to God in prayer!

We should make sure that we do not carry our burdens on our own. God wants us to cast every care and concern on him because he cares for us.

APRIL 20

The Crippled Woman
Luke 13:10-13

The poor woman had been crippled for eighteen years. Her body was bent and disfigured. The Lord Jesus changed her life in a moment, setting her free from her pain and disability. Her immediate response was to glorify God, praising him for his goodness to her.

Chico is an Apurina Indian living in the jungle of Brazil. For many years he and his tribes-people were bound by the power of sin; killing and cannibalism were second nature to them. Then missionaries came to Monkey Village, learned and wrote the language and translated God's Word.

Chico and some others were set free from the power of Satan and their lives were changed. Now Chico wants to glorify God's name too. One day he paddled in his canoe for one and a half hours to the next village to ask a friend to come with him to a service to hear God's Word. His days are filled with worshipping God and speaking about him and his Word.

We can praise God too in many ways. We can remember to thank him when we recover from illness. We should do what we can for the Lord in gratitude, for he has done so much for us.

APRIL 21

Queen Of Sheba

Matthew 12:42

Jesus spoke very plainly and directly in condemning sin and telling people why he came to the world. Many of the people who saw and heard him were hard-hearted and disbelieving.

Jesus used the story of the Queen of Sheba coming to visit Solomon to drive home his point. The queen travelled many miles to ask hard questions of wise King Solomon and to tell him all that was on her mind. She was absolutely overwhelmed by what she saw and heard.

'The Queen of the South will condemn you,' said Jesus to the people. 'You do not realise that someone greater than Solomon is in your midst.'

The Queen of Sheba made a great effort to see Solomon. The people to whom Jesus was speaking made no effort at all to contact the Son of God who was living among them. Indeed they despised him and rejected him.

We should take care that the Queen of Sheba will not condemn us also. The Word of God is near us. Let us not despise and reject it, but rather value it and be willing to make a great effort to hear its wisdom - the wisdom of the one who is greater than Solomon.

APRIL 22

Mary's Alabaster Box
Matthew 26:6-13; John 12:1-8

A dinner was given in Jesus' honour when he visited Bethany. Mary came to this feast with her most precious possession. This was an expensive casket of perfumed ointment which she broke open and poured over Jesus' head as he sat at a meal.

What is the most precious thing that we possess? Jesus says, 'What good is it for a man to gain the whole world, yet forfeit his soul?' We have nothing more valuable than our soul, so he wants us to give that to him.

Mary was criticised for what she did. 'What a waste!' the disciples said. 'The ointment could have been sold and the money given to poor people.' That sounded very reasonable. Their motive was good too - they were showing care and concern for the poor.

But they were rebuked, for Jesus told them that Mary's motive was even higher. She gave this ointment for the glory of her Saviour and to show how much she loved him. Jesus was glad that Mary showed such love.

He told the disciples that wherever the gospel would be preached, people would hear of what she had done, and the fact that we are thinking about Mary today proves that to be true.

APRIL 23

Women At The Cross
Matthew 27:55-56

A minister in the Highlands of Scotland many years ago heard that some ladies in his congregation were gathering in a certain house to have a prayer-meeting. At that time and in that culture it was not at all usual for women to pray aloud in public, so the minister was a bit dubious about this gathering.

He went to the lady whose home was used for the meeting and asked if he might come secretly and listen to what was going on. The lady allowed the minister to sit in the cupboard under the stairs, and the prayer-meeting went ahead.

After the ladies had gone home, the minister came out of his hiding-place. 'What have you to say now?' he was asked. 'I have never heard such expressions of love to my Saviour before,' he replied. No more doubts about the prayer-meeting!

When Jesus was suffering such agony on the cross at Calvary, the women folk were expressing their love to him in an open way. Mary Magdalene and others had often ministered to him. Now at his death they stood some distance away watching in sympathy, and no doubt praying.

Let us show our love for him in whatever way we can.

APRIL 24

Women At The Sepulchre
Matthew 28:1-10

Jesus had died and Mary Magdalene and another woman, also called Mary, came to look at the grave. They must have been sad and distressed, wondering what was happening. But the women were to witness still more momentous events. The earth shook, the stone rolled away from the grave, and an angel appeared and spoke to them. 'Don't be afraid,' he said. 'I know you are looking for Jesus. He is not here. He has risen.'

How these words must have cheered their hearts! Everything was not finished. Jesus was alive again!

They could not keep the great news to themselves. They had to share it. Full of emotion - apprehension and joy - they ran off to tell the disciples the news.

Even better was to come. On the way they met Jesus himself. 'Greetings!' he said, and they bowed down and worshipped him.

When we hear the good news of the risen Lord Jesus, do we keep it to ourselves or do we, like the women, want to share it with others? If we do, then there is a greater blessing for ourselves too. When the women went to tell others, they met Jesus himself. When we go to others with his Word, Jesus has promised to be with us.

APRIL 25

Dorcas With The Helping Hand
Acts 9:36-43

There is something very special about receiving a gift that has been made by the giver because it conveys to us the giver's love and care.

Dorcas was always busy helping others. She was good with her hands and made garments for needy families in Joppa; so when she became ill and died, what distress the people felt! Peter the apostle was sent for. Could he restore Dorcas to life?

After the widows had shown the different clothes that Dorcas had made for them, Peter put them all out of the room and prayed. Then he spoke to the dead woman and miraculously Dorcas was restored to life. He took her hand and helped her to her feet. Imagine the rejoicing when Dorcas was again introduced to her friends!

Peter performed this miracle, not that he would be praised, but that God would have the glory. Many people were convinced of the truth of the gospel as a result and believed in the Lord.

Dorcas' sewing was one link in the chain to draw many people to the Lord Jesus. This should encourage us to do any small act of kindness. God may use that in his purpose of mercy to one of his people.

APRIL 26

Rhoda And The Visitor
Acts 12:11-17

Rhoda was a servant in a Christian home in Jerusalem. Times were very anxious. Peter the preacher was in prison, under threat of death. Many Christians met in this home during the crisis and their fervent prayer was that Peter would be released.

Then a knock came on the outer door. Rhoda was sent to see who was there at this late hour, and to her amazement the voice replying to her call was Peter's. She was so taken aback that instead of opening the door for him, she ran back into the room to tell the great news to the others. No one believed her. 'You are mad,' was the first reaction. 'It can't be him.'

Peter continued knocking at the door and eventually someone had the sense to open up for him. Peter, indeed, was standing before them - the answer to their prayer.

How slow they were to believe that God had answered their prayer! Are we sometimes like that? We might pray earnestly for something and yet be surprised and even disbelieving when God grants our request. How much better to be like David the Psalmist who after he prayed said that he 'waited in expectation'! (Psalm 5:3).

APRIL 27

Lydia - On The Lord's Business

Acts 16:14-15, 40

'I am always so busy I never get enough time to pray.' That is often how the busy housewife or career woman feels. Not so with Lydia. She was a very active businesswoman selling textiles, but she still found time regularly to attend a prayer-meeting at the river-side in Philippi. It was there that she heard Paul the missionary preach.

The message of Paul changed her life. Her conversion was not dramatic but the Lord opened her heart.

The love of Jesus in Lydia's heart had an effect on her life. She wanted to show her love to the Lord by serving him, and she did this by showing her loving concern for Paul and his friends - persuading them to stay at her home for a while.

What effect does the love of Jesus have in our lives? Do we show our love by serving him? 'What can I do?' we may say.

God's servants need our caring concern. That can mean praying for them regularly or helping them practically. If our position means that we cannot do very much, Jesus is pleased with our service, even if all we can give is a cup of cold water.

APRIL 28

Priscilla - More Than A Tentmaker
Acts 18:1-4, 18-27

We often feel an admiration for people who travel a lot - perhaps even making their home in several different countries. Our admiration is even greater when we hear of people going to new countries to work for the Lord. Some people give up the comforts of home to carry on their profession in a foreign country with the purpose of building up a Christian church and opening their homes to further the gospel. We sometimes call these people 'tentmaker' missionaries.

Priscilla and her husband Aquila were the original tentmaker missionaries. When they were forced to leave Rome they settled in Corinth, working as tentmakers but helping the church, especially Paul when he too came there to preach. Later they moved on to Ephesus to help found the church there, and one day they heard Apollos preaching in the synagogue. He was learned, a fervent preacher who taught the people about the Lord Jesus, but on some aspects of doctrine he was deficient.

Priscilla and Aquila, recognising this weakness in his preaching, invited him into their home and, while showing him this hospitality, explained to him the way of God more adequately. Apollos greatly benefited from this and his preaching proved to be a blessing to many.

APRIL 29

Phoebe - The Helper
Romans 16:1-2

Every Christian has some talent to use for the Lord Jesus. God requires our service in whatever way we are able. Some ladies may make the excuse, 'I am just a woman. What can I do?'

We should learn from Phoebe who was highly commended by Paul as a servant of the church. There may be some question as to what 'servant' means but she had clearly been a help to many people, including Paul himself, and she was probably entrusted with the delivery of Paul's letter to the Roman church.

How many things we can do for our fellow Christians, even in our own home!

A sympathetic listening ear is a very valuable gift to have, as is the ability to give wise advice when asked. A letter of encouragement or a phone-call just to say 'I am thinking of you' - these can be gifts of untold value.

Jesus notices these actions. 'Whatever you did for one of the least of these brothers of mine, you did for me,' he said. If we want to give service to Jesus, then we should show kindness to his followers. The greatest work that we can do is to pray for the church and for the preachers of the gospel.

APRIL 30

MAY

SHIRLEY LEES

*Why Does God
Permit Suffering?*

Suffering

Consider it pure joy, my brothers, whenever you face trials of many kinds, because you know that the testing of your faith develops perseverance. Perseverance must finish its work so that you may be mature and complete... (James 1:2-4).

How can we count trials as joy? Or how can they be 'friends' as in J B Phillips' translation? 'When all kinds of trials and temptation crowd into your lives, my brothers, don't resent them as intruders but welcome them as friends.'

Our little handicapped daughter gave us much joy but also much sadness. When she was about five, we heard a preacher who, referring to the stereotype of a Scotsman, said, 'Be Scots with your suffering. Don't waste a penny of it.' We have never forgotten it. It reminds us to make full use of our sufferings by allowing them to make us 'mature and complete' rather than letting bitterness stunt our spiritual growth.

This month we are going to study the effects of suffering on three people in the Old Testament. Firstly Joseph whom God moulded by his sufferings; then Habakkuk as he reacted to God's forthcoming chastisement of his people; finally we will contemplate the innocent sufferings of Job.

MAY 1

Joseph

Joseph, a young man of seventeen, was tending the flocks with his brothers...Now Israel loved Joseph more than any of his other sons...and he made a richly ornamented robe for him. When his brothers saw that their father loved him more than any of them, they hated him (Gen. 37:2-4).

God chose Joseph to be part of his loving purposes in saving and moulding the nation of Israel through whom the Saviour of the world was to come.

What unlikely material he chose! Born of a father whose very name, Jacob, spoke of his crooked nature, and a mother, Rachel, who stole from her father and then sweetly lied to cover up her sin, Joseph was also spoilt. He has been described as 'the most objectionable young prig that ever strutted around in a long-sleeved coat'.

But God had chosen him. He would have to suffer a great deal before he knew what God was doing with his life, but he would learn that 'the God of all grace...after you have suffered a little while, will himself restore you and make you strong, firm and steadfast' (1 Peter 5:10).

However unsuitable we feel, God can mould us and use us in his service. He will not let us suffer in vain.

MAY 2

The Best Is Still True

Joseph went after his brothers....'Here comes that dreamer!' they said to each other...'Let's kill him....Then we'll see what comes of his dreams.' When Reuben heard this, he tried to rescue him... (Gen. 37:17-21).

Joseph's dreams were God-given, no doubt to help him through the thirteen years of pain and suffering he was going to endure, but he would have been wise not to have taunted his older brothers with them. Their resentment built up day after day until one day it boiled over. In the remoteness of the Judean hills, they stripped him of the hated robe, symbol of his father's favouritism, and threw him into an empty pit.

Joseph's cosy world fell apart. As he pleaded for his life he must have wondered (as did his brothers) what was going to come of his dreams. They could not know that this was a step towards their fulfilment. Joseph was to learn that, though the worst had happened, the best (God's love and care for him) was still true.

For us too when the worst happens, the best is still true. God will never stop loving us. In that love, he may allow bad things to happen. But he will not let us go.

Transformed

Potiphar, an Egyptian who was one of Pharaoh's officials...bought [Joseph]...The LORD was with Joseph and he prospered (Gen. 39:1-2).

It was not by chance that Potiphar noticed a good-looking young Hebrew slave in the market-place and bought him. God had a dual purpose in allowing Joseph to be taken as a slave to Egypt. He was to be in the right place at the right time to save God's chosen people from famine. He also needed to be the right sort of person with the right sort of skills to do that.

In Potiphar's service Joseph responded to God as he moulded, changed and trained him. He did not go around licking his wounds and grudgingly doing what he had to do. He presumably learnt the language, worked hard and became a reliable person. So much so that Potiphar was content to put him in charge of his whole household because he 'saw that the LORD was with him and that the LORD gave him success in everything he did.'

To be 'transformed into his likeness with ever-increasing glory' may not be a comfortable process but it is one which we will look back on with gratitude when we meet the Lord.

MAY 4

'A Lucky Fellow'

The LORD was with Joseph and he prospered ... Joseph's master took him and put him in prison, the place where the king's prisoners were confined...The LORD was with Joseph and gave him success in whatever he did (Gen. 39:2,20,23).

According to an old English translation of the Bible, 'the Lord was with Joseph and he was a lucky fellow.' We would not call it luck to be bought as a slave, unjustly accused and thrown into prison - not a clean, comfortable twentieth-century Western prison but slow, deadly destruction in shackles in an Eastern dungeon. Hardly appropriate, we would feel, even to hint at any good luck attached to that.

In all the injustice and misery meted out to him, could Joseph believe that he was 'lucky'? Did God still love him? Yes, he did; and we can be encouraged that God can bring good out of the evil of any injustice or suffering which we are enduring. There is a wonderful little twist to the story which demonstrates God's over-ruling control. Had Joseph not been put in 'the place where the king's prisoners were confined', then he would never have come to Pharaoh's attention.

God's loving purposes were not thwarted, rather furthered, in Joseph's sufferings.

MAY 5

Disappointed

Pharaoh was angry with his two officials...and put them ...in the same prison where Joseph was confined... [Pharaoh] restored the chief cupbearer ...The chief cupbearer, however, did not remember Joseph; he forgot him (Gen. 40:2-4,21,23).

Disappointment! We have all experienced it. Someone, something, has let us down. Promises have been broken, and with Solomon we feel that 'hope deferred makes the heart sick'. We may be tempted to bitterness, depression, even anger against God.

Joseph knew the pain of disappointment. He saw God's hand in his being prospered in prison and in the wisdom he received to interpret the dreams of Pharaoh's officials. No doubt he thought he saw God working for his release when the cupbearer was restored to office. Instead he was to suffer two more years before God brought him out with his faith strengthened and his character developed to undertake his heavy responsibilities.

Do we 'waste' our disappointments or see them as the opportunity to have our faith strengthened? Gold, if it could feel, would prefer not to go through the fire, but when it has done it comes out pure. Our disappointments can be the fire that refines our faith.

MAY 6

Strong In God

Pharaoh said to Joseph, 'I had a dream, and no one can interpret it. But I have heard it said of you that when you hear a dream you can interpret it.' 'I cannot do it,' Joseph replied ... 'but God will give Pharaoh the answer he desires' (Gen. 41:15-16).

A quick shave (Egyptians did not like beards), a wash and a change of clothing, and Joseph was brought before Pharaoh. From the dinginess of the dungeon he was brought out into the bright light of Pharaoh's court. It was enough to turn any young man's head, especially one who had had dreams of grandeur. But it was also a terrifying experience. Joseph knew all too well that the baker had been killed on a whim.

What had he learnt in thirteen years of slavery and imprisonment? Amongst other things, courage, humility and an awareness of God. Standing before Pharaoh, he disclaimed all magical powers and cleverness and gave all the glory to God. 'I cannot do it, but God will.'

Paul went to the Corinthians 'in weakness and fear and with much trembling...but with a demonstration of the Spirit's power' (1 Cor. 2:3-4). However weak, however fearful, however inadequate we feel, we can be strong in God.

MAY 7

God's Great Purpose

Pharaoh said to Joseph, 'Since God has made all this known to you, there is no one so discerning and wise as you. You shall be in charge of my palace, and all my people are to submit to your orders. Only with respect to the throne will I be greater than you' (Gen. 41:39-40).

Freedom and recognition at last! Is that what it is all about? There are those in the prosperous West who would have us believe that health and prosperity can be expected if we truly follow the Lord. But God had not rescued Joseph just to give him and his family material prosperity.

When man fell, God had promised that the seed of the woman would crush the serpent's head. In order to fulfil that promise, he called Abraham and his family. Joseph's story is part of that remarkable history which was to culminate (in spite of all Satan's efforts through the centuries to hinder it) in the coming of Jesus. Joseph was made ruler of Egypt in order to keep God's family alive.

Our lives may seem very insignificant. But God has a great purpose for each one of us in furthering his kingdom, whether it is in health or sickness, prosperity or suffering.

MAY 8

Willingness To Forgive

Joseph said to his brothers, 'Come close to me...I am your brother Joseph, the one you sold into Egypt! And now, do not be distressed and do not be angry with yourselves for selling me here, because it was to save lives that God sent me ahead of you' (Gen. 45:4-5).

If Joseph had been harbouring resentment through all those hard years in Egypt, how easy it would have been to use his position of power to get his own back on his brothers for their despicable behaviour! But no. He reminds them of their sin but does not demand an apology before calling them, through his tears, to 'come close'. This is not the behaviour of a bitter man. Joseph has learnt to trust God and to forgive those who have caused his sufferings.

Sometimes when we have been badly hurt, an apology puts things right. That is good. There are other times when we have to realise that we have no right to demand an apology before restoring good relations. If we do not want our lives to be ruined by a 'root of bitterness' we must genuinely forgive and 'come close' in love, trusting God to work in those who have hurt us.

MAY 9

But God

'For two years now there has been famine in the land, and for the next five years there will not be ploughing...But God sent me ahead of you...to save your lives... So then, it was not you who sent me here, but God' (Gen. 45:6-8).

But God! Joseph repeats these words after Jacob's death. 'You intended to harm me, but God intended it for good' (Gen. 50:20). Stephen takes up the same point in his great defence in Acts: 'The patriarchs...sold him (Joseph) as a slave into Egypt. But God was with him and rescued him' (Acts 7:9-10).

'But God' sustained Joseph during those thirteen long years of suffering. He continued to believe that God was in control. How else could he have greeted his brothers without bitterness or rancour?

Wang Ming Dao, the Chinese pastor, who suffered twenty-two years of the deprivation and cruelty of a Chinese communist jail, had the same belief in God's sovereignty. Imprisoned unjustly for his stand as a Christian, he came away from there without bitterness and with his faith in God stronger than before. 'I met God in prison,' he said.

Can we think back and praise God for the situations in our lives where 'But God...' has sustained us?

MAY 10

Habakkuk And God's Silence

How long, O LORD, must I call for help, but you do not listen? Or cry out to you, 'Violence!' but you do not save? (Hab. 1:2).

The prophet Habakkuk, contemporary of Jeremiah, lived at a time of moral and spiritual decline in Judah. He knew that God had chosen his people and he knew too that many a time when they had backslidden, God had anointed a prophet to call them back to obedience and true worship.

He was one of those prophets. But he had been praying and praying and God didn't seem to be doing anything. He came to God with his problem but God was silent.

Have we not all, at some time, stood where Habakkuk stood? We have prayed earnestly for something for days, weeks, months, even years, and God remains silent. We are tempted to think that he has not heard us. He has, but maybe he wants us to learn to trust him in the silence and realise that prayer is not a 'divine slot-machine'. God knows when it is best to answer.

Let us think back to occasions in our lives when our faith has been tested and strengthened and we have come closer to God in the silence.

MAY 11

Being Honest With God

O LORD...why do you make me look at injustice?
Why do you tolerate wrong? Destruction and violence
are before me...The wicked hem in the righteous, so that
justice is perverted (Hab. 1:2-4).

One of the lovely things about the little book of
Habakkuk is its honesty. Habakkuk is no plastic saint.
He has a complaint about God's dealings with him and
his people, and he is not afraid to tell God about it.

When we were working in a pioneer missionary
situation, one of our little girls was very unhappy in
her first year at boarding-school. I blamed God for
putting us in that situation and told him I hated him!
Of course I quickly realised what an outrageous thing
I had done. I repented and God lovingly gave me a
wonderful sense of his forgiveness.

Habakkuk too was saying outrageous things. He
was questioning God's sovereignty, his holiness, his
willingness to answer prayer. God did not rebuke him
for his honesty, but rather changed his heart.

When we are hurt, instead of grumbling to others, it
is good to come honestly to God and to tell him what
we are feeling. He knows anyway and he has told us
to 'cast all our anxiety on him' (1 Peter 5:7).

MAY 12

God's Mysterious Ways

Look at the nations and watch and be utterly amazed... I am raising up the Babylonians, that ruthless and impetuous people, who sweep across the whole earth to seize dwelling places not their own (Hab. 1:5-6).

Habakkuk had in effect questioned whether God was really in control of his world. God's unexpected and incredible reply showed that he was. He was going to use the Babylonians to chasten his chosen people.

Whether it is in our personal lives or on the wider canvas of history, God sometimes answers our prayers in unexpected and unwished-for ways. Some situations may have to get worse before they can get better.

My daughter once complained to me that God seemed to be putting her into a series of circumstances where she struggled to trust him. 'Have you by any chance been asking God to give you more patience in trusting him?' I asked. 'Oh dear, yes I have,' she replied!

William Cooper reminds us that 'God moves in a mysterious way' and we must

> 'Trust him for his grace
> Behind a frowning providence
> He hides a smiling face.'

MAY 13

The Lord, My Holy One

O LORD, are you not from everlasting? My God, my Holy One, we will not die. O LORD, you have appointed them to execute judgement; O Rock, you have ordained them to punish (Hab. 1:12).

Habakkuk was 'utterly amazed' at God's reply. Can we imagine how devastated we would have felt in his situation? But we can learn a very wise strategy from Habakkuk. Before stating his second complaint, he steps back from his problem and reminds himself who God is.

When LORD is written in capital letters in our Bibles, it translates Yahweh - the God of the covenant. Yahweh is the eternal, creator God. He is almighty. He is also 'my God, my Holy One'. Habakkuk belongs to him. There will be suffering as God 'executes judgment' but he will not abandon his chosen people. He is the Rock - utterly, absolutely reliable. However bad the news, Habakkuk can trust God.

Habakkuk helps us to react to bad news, whether international, national or personal. We too can trust God, as we put our problem into the context of his faithfulness and covenant-keeping love.

Are there issues worrying us where we need to step back for a while and see them against the wider canvas of Yahweh's presence?

Watching In Confidence

Your eyes are too pure to look on evil; you cannot tolerate wrong... Why are you silent while the wicked swallow up those more righteous than themselves?... I will stand at my watch... I will look to see what he will say to me... (Hab. 1:13; 2:1).

Once again Habakkuk reminded himself of things that were certain. He had no doubt that God was holy and just. He knew that God would never act in an unfair or unjust way. But this led him to a further dilemma. How could such a holy God use as his instrument the ruthless Babylonians whose cruelty and power had struck fear into all the peoples around?

Reassured by his contemplation of the character of God, Habakkuk was prepared to leave the matter with him. No longer complaining about God's silence, he would 'stand at his watch' in faith and wait expectantly for God to answer.

When we find ourselves going round in circles as we pray, it is good to leave our dilemmas with God. We can be confident that he has heard and we can wait expectantly, not needing to pester him with our request, nor forgetting all about it, but knowing that God will answer in his own time.

MAY 15

God's Perfect Timing

Then the LORD replied: 'Write down the revelation ... for [it] awaits an appointed time; it speaks of the end and will not prove false. Though it linger, wait for it; it will certainly come and will not delay' (Hab. 2:2-3).

God's timing is perfect and his prophecies will not 'prove false'. God heard Habakkuk's prayer and in chapter 2 he explained the future destruction of the Babylonians. History records that they were soon defeated by the Medo-Persian empire.

God's timing was perfect too when he fulfilled the promise of a Saviour in Genesis 3. Paul tells us that 'when the time had fully come, God sent his Son' (Gal. 4:4). The coming of Jesus was at exactly God's time. It had not been delayed by Satan's efforts to destroy the royal line through which he came.

Was not even the Roman empire part of God's plan? The gospel was able to spread rapidly, unhindered by language (Greek was universal), helped by Roman roads and Roman law (to which Paul was able to appeal), and even Greek philosophy had opened the minds of men and women to receive new things.

As we wait for Jesus to bring peace and justice, let us remind ourselves that kings, empires, nations, are all in God's hands.

MAY 16

By Faith

The righteous will live by his faith (Hab. 2:4).

Habakkuk must have wondered how much suffering he and his people would have to endure before God fulfilled his promise. Hence the need to remind him that 'the righteous will live by his faith.' God answered Habakkuk's prayer as he spelt out the revelation in the five woes which he pronounced. The immediate fulfilment was that Babylon's triumph was going to be short-lived. We too can take encouragement from these verses. Not only is God in control of world history but everything that is evil is under his ultimate judgment.

But that is not all. God promised that 'the earth shall be filled with the glory of God as the waters cover the sea.' There is no indication as to how or when this will happen, just that it will. Faith must be exercised in continuing to believe it. As we witness in our immediate surroundings or as we think of the church's world-wide missionary endeavours, we are given the confidence to know that God's promises will be fulfilled. 'At the name of Jesus, every knee shall bow' (Phil. 2:10).

Let us stop to pray for someone we know who is involved in God's missionary programme, whether at home or abroad.

MAY 17

God On The Throne

Of what value is an idol, since a man has carved it?... For he who makes it trusts in his own creation; ... But the LORD is in his holy temple; let all the earth be silent before him (Hab. 2:18,20).

What a contrast! The Babylonians trusted in their man-made idols. God Almighty, Habakkuk's God, is on his throne, ruling the universe which he has himself created.

In what do we put our trust? Do we hope in idols or do we 'live by faith'? Even we Christians can some-times feel that prosperity, orthodoxy or mere activity are more reliable than faith in an unseen God.

God says to us as he said to Habakkuk, 'God is God. Let all the earth be silent before him,' whether it is the voice of human self-sufficiency or the agonised ques-tioning of God's own people fearing he has lost con-trol of his world! We will find with Habakkuk that as we worship God he gives us a fresh assurance that our day-by-day faith rests in the great 'I am'.

'You are worthy, our Lord and God,
    to receive glory and honour and power,
for you created all things,
    and by your will they were created
    and have their being' (Rev. 4:11).

Wrath And Mercy

LORD, I have heard of your fame; I stand in awe of your deeds, O LORD. Renew them in our day, in our time make them known; in wrath remember mercy (Hab. 3:2).

Habakkuk responded to God's call to silent obedience and worship. As he came in humble adoration, he was filled with awe at God's mighty power and unspeakable holiness. He was now more concerned for God's work than for his own well-being. He recognised that the sin both of Judah and the Babylonians was such that God would be utterly just if he destroyed both. Habakkuk had however experienced another side to God's character. He knew that he cared for his people, and so asked that God would remember his mercy in the midst of his justifiable wrath.

If we are to keep calm in adversity, we must maintain a balanced understanding of the character of God. Some think only of his holiness, his wrath and his awesome power. God becomes an ogre. Others think only of his love, his mercy, his grace, and God becomes like a heavenly grandfather. Either view by itself leads us astray; together we are assured that God can be trusted to do right in all circumstances, whatever they may be.

MAY 19

Count Your Blessings

You came out to deliver your people, to save your anointed one ... I heard and my heart pounded, my lips quivered at the sound ... Yet I will wait patiently for the day of calamity to come on the nation invading us (Hab. 3:13,16).

As Habakkuk prayed, he was reminded of all the good things that God had done for his people in the past. In praise to God he listed many of the miracles that God had performed as he 'came out to deliver'. Habakkuk learnt afresh to trust God. Although he was not ashamed to say he was terrified by the prospect of a Babylonian invasion, he would wait patiently for God to chasten Judah and fulfil his promise of ultimate judgment on the Babylonians. What a transformed Habakkuk we see as the result of his meeting with God!

Recalling God's interventions in the history of Israel helped him to face the future. We too can gain strength from 'counting our blessings'. As we list some of God's goodnesses to us, we will be greatly encouraged to trust him for the future.

God My Saviour

Though the fig-tree does not bud and there are no grapes on the vines, though the olive crop fails and the fields produce no food, though there are no sheep in the pen and no cattle in the stalls, yet I will rejoice in the LORD, I will be joyful in God my Saviour (Hab. 3:17-18).

Prayer does not change God but it does change us (and Habakkuk). Thomson in *The Praying Christ* writes: 'The aim of prayer is not to make God change his will but to enable us to change our mind and disposition and thus allow him to do for us and through us what he cannot do until we are fully yielded to him.'

In these verses we see the triumph of Habakkuk the man of faith. He has brought his complaints to God and God has answered him. He does not bury his head in the sand. He has heard of the 'scorched earth' policy of the Babylonians but, as he has prayed, his faith has grown. He will trust God, however much suffering he and his people will have to endure. And in the midst of suffering he will keep God his Saviour central in his thinking.

MAY 21

BitternessAndAcceptance

The Sovereign LORD is my strength; he makes my feet like the feet of a deer, he enables me to go on the heights (Hab. 3:19).

Habakkuk started in a state of arguing and complaining depression, doubting God's justice and even his ability to control his world. He ended, in the face of devastating suffering, expressing exciting confidence in God as he pictured himself as a deer leaping from rock to rock up in the high mountains. Is it possible that this can happen to us?

There are two ways in which we can react to suffering when God appears unwilling to alleviate it. As we come with our agonising questions to God, we can either allow ourselves to think that God does not love us because he has not intervened, or we can do what Habakkuk did and accept God's way. In the security of knowing that our relationship with God is firmly based on the foundation of God's promises, we can experience the strength which God, the Sovereign Lord, supplies.

'God is faithful; he will not let you be tempted [tested] beyond what you can bear. But when you are tempted, he will also provide a way out, so that you can stand up under it' (1 Cor. 10:13).

MAY 22

Job Refined By Fire

In the land of Uz there lived a man whose name was Job. This man was blameless and upright; he feared God and shunned evil (Job 1:1).

Job was a devout, godly man. There is no doubt about his innocence. God himself says, 'There is no one on earth like him. He is blameless and upright, a man who fears God and shuns evil' (1:8).

In these days when there are many telling us that if we have faith we can expect to be healed of all our sicknesses, it is important to remember that it was God who said that Job was blameless. Yes, God does heal. Job, however, was a godly man who suffered appallingly before God eventually healed him.

Some suffering is the consequence of our disobedience as in the case of the Jewish people of Habakkuk's day. Some suffering is preparation for future ministry as in the case of Joseph. But some suffering may come to people like Job who have a strong faith in God.

'These [trials] have come so that your faith - of greater worth than gold, which perishes even though refined by fire - may be proved genuine and may result in praise, glory and honour when Jesus Christ is revealed' (1 Peter 1:7).

MAY 23

For God's Sake

The LORD said to Satan, 'Have you considered my servant Job? There is no one on earth like him...' 'Does Job fear God for nothing?' Satan replied. 'Have you not put a hedge around him and his household and everything he has?...But stretch out your hand and strike everything he has, and he will surely curse you to your face' (Job 1:8-11).

In the prologue to the book of Job, we witness an encounter between God and Satan. God challenged Satan to look at the godliness of his servant Job. 'Does Job fear God for nothing?' Satan sneered in reply. He refused to accept that Job served God for God's sake but rather for what he could get out of him.

Do we, albeit unconsciously, serve God for what we can get out of him? Do we love the gifts more than the giver? We rejoice in God's care and protection (and rightly so) but are we ever in danger of looking on this as a sort of insurance policy against the evil and suffering in the world? When things go wrong we then blame God for letting us down.

Let us ask God to help us to love him even when he withholds his gifts for a while.

MAY 24

Confidence In God

The LORD said to Satan, 'Very well, then, everything he has is in your hands, but on the man himself do not lay a finger.'

Job got up and tore his robe and shaved his head. Then he fell to the ground in worship and said... 'The LORD gave and the LORD has taken away; may the name of the LORD be praised' (Job 1:12, 20-21).

It is clear, from the viewpoint of heaven, that God was in control. He decided how far Satan could go. Given this permission, Satan went out from God's presence and in one day destroyed all Job's livestock, servants and family.

What a remarkable man Job was! He grieved deeply but accepted God's control over all things. At this point he didn't even ask 'Why?' but fell to the ground in worship, acknowledging that all that he had came from God. He did not know what had gone on between God and Satan, but he held fast to his confidence in God.

Job's faith enabled him to trust God in the deepest depths of grief. Are we willing to ask God to help us to trust him in the darkness and mystery of suffering, even though, with Job, we can see no reasonable explanation for it?

MAY 25

Tested Still Further

The LORD said to Satan... '[Job] still maintains his
integrity, though you incited me against him to ruin him
without any reason.'

Satan replied... 'But stretch out your hand and strike
his flesh and bones and he will surely curse you to your
face.'

The LORD said to Satan, '... He is in your hands; but
you must spare his life' (Job 2:3,5-6).

Job's reaction to this piling on of suffering was one of
remarkable acceptance. 'Shall we accept good from
God, and not trouble?'

God had such confidence that Job would react like that,
that he was prepared to allow him to be tested still further.
Through Job's endurance he would demonstrate to Satan
that his servant would continue to worship him, even
though the extent of his suffering was almost unbearable.
God allowed Job to come very near the brink of his
endurance. But he finally saw him through the blackness
of despair to ultimate peace. Some of us may wonder if
God is taking us too near the brink. But he has promised
to give us the strength needed to meet every situation.

'Your strength will equal your days...The eternal
God is your refuge, and underneath are the everlasting
arms' (Deut. 33:25,27).

MAY 26

True Friendship

Job's three friends ... set out from their homes ... to go and sympathise with him and comfort him. When they saw him from a distance, they could hardly recognise him; they began to weep aloud...Then they sat on the ground with him for seven days and seven nights. No one said a word to him, because they saw how great his suffering was (Job 2:11-13).

Whatever we think of Job's friends, they were true friends at the beginning. Even his poor wife, probably blinded by her own agony and sense of helplessness, had added to his misery by encouraging him to do just what Satan wanted him to do. 'Are you still holding on to your integrity?' she queried. 'Curse God and die!'

The friends came and 'sat where he sat' alone among the ashes, weeping with genuine distress and sharing with him in quiet solitude. It was not a time to try to find answers but a time to show that they cared.

There are times when sorrow is too deep for words. However helpless we feel, true companionship will be willing to share rather than rush into finding glib answers.

Is there anyone we know who could do with a visit or a phone-call today?

MAY 27

The Kinsman-Redeemer

God's terrors are marshalled against me... I loathe my very life; therefore I will give free rein to my complaint and speak out in the bitterness of my soul... If only there were someone to arbitrate between us... I know that my Redeemer lives... I myself will see him with my own eyes (Job 6:4; 10:1; 9:33; 19:25,27).

After the silence, Job burst out in agony of soul, cursing the day he was born. Then came the questioning, depression and anger. Because of his firm belief that 'to God belong wisdom and power' his anger was inevitably directed against God. Why, why had God allowed this? he asked, as so many of us have done.

In spite of his depression, which almost (but not quite) led him to say that God was not good, he held on in faith. 'Though he slay me, yet will I hope in him' (13:15). Not knowing anything of the cross of Christ, he expressed his confidence in his Kinsman-Redeemer (Heb. go'el).

We know that Jesus is that 'Kinsman-Redeemer'. However dark our lives, we have the assurance that he is there with us and we can say with Job, 'He knows the way that I take; when he has tested me, I shall come forth as gold' (23:10).

MAY 28

Sowing And Reaping

Who, being innocent, has ever perished?... those who plough evil and those who sow trouble reap it... if you put away the sin that is in your hand... then you will lift up your face without shame (Job 4:7-8; 11:14-15).

Job and his friends rightly believed in the moral basis of the world that God had created; but faced with the inexplicable, Job battled to maintain his relationship with God, while his friends looked for a neat explanation. They believed that if they obeyed God, he would bless them. If they disobeyed God he would punish them. Job therefore must have sinned.

Job knew he was a sinner (hence the burnt offerings) but he knew his suffering was not related to his sin. The friends had part of the truth - 'as you sow you reap' - but if that were the whole truth, then we would do good purely out of selfish motives. That is what Satan claimed. But God was demonstrating that Job served him because he loved him, even when he allowed him to suffer.

At the Cross, the simple law of 'as you sow you reap' was both fulfilled and superseded by grace. Christ suffered for us, reaping what we had sown, purely because he loves us.

MAY 29

The Lord's Answer

The LORD answered Job out of the storm (Job 38:1).

At last Job had his wish. What had made his suffering so terrible was God's silence and distance. Now he speaks. He does not explain about Satan's wager. Instead we have a glorious description of God in his creative versatility. He is God Almighty who rules the world with wisdom, power and justice but we cannot always understand his ways.

Are we disappointed? Job was not. He knew that God had been there in the darkness. When he saw the Lord he was satisfied and could leave the mysteries with him.

The book of Job does not give us answers as to why a God of love allows suffering in his world. It tells us that faith enables us to live with loose ends and seeming contradictions.

One day a friend suggested we could ask the Lord, when we saw him in heaven, why he allowed our little girl to be handicapped. Then I read John 16:22-23: 'Now you are going through pain, but I will see you again and your hearts will thrill with joy - the joy no one can take away from you - and on that day you will not ask me any questions.' There will be no need.

MAY 30

Job's Prayer For His Friends

After the LORD had said these things to Job, he said to Eliphaz the Temanite, 'I am angry with you and your two friends, because you have not spoken of me what is right, as my servant Job has ... My servant Job will pray for you and I will accept his prayer ...' After Job had prayed for his friends, the LORD made him prosperous again (Job 42:7-8,10).

Release at last. Job had reached the end of the tunnel through which God in his wisdom had allowed him to pass. Verse 10 in the A.V. reads, 'The LORD turned the captivity of Job, when he prayed for his friends.' He had been a captive to his pain and suffering. He had been a captive to his anger against God and his friends. And, not unnaturally, he had been very preoccupied with himself.

God told him to turn his eyes away from himself and to pray for his friends who had hurt him. Then he answered far beyond his asking by releasing Job himself.

When we are ill, depressed, bereaved, we often feel beyond the ability to pray even for ourselves. But we will be amazed at the encouragement God gives us if we can momentarily turn our eyes outward and pray for someone else.

MAY 31

JUNE

PHILIP HACKING

The God Of The Living Hope

The God Squad
1 Peter 1:1-2

This is an interesting portrait gallery. Clearly Peter can be seen here. The letter bears many marks of his reminiscences of Jesus. He begins with his correct title reminding us that he speaks with authority as an apostle. But our Lord is in the centre of the picture. Four times in the first three verses his full title is given.

This letter was written at an hour when persecution was beginning in the reign of Nero. There is the beginning of a hint in verse 6, but wonderfully Peter begins not with the troubles but with the provision of God for Christians scattered throughout the world.

In the portrait gallery are Christians who are seen as 'strangers in the world'. Genuine believers do not belong to the present world. But in the providence of God Christians are scattered, so that they might be an influence of salt and light. These Christians were in a very wealthy part of the Roman Empire, but there was much spiritual poverty there.

In the portrait gallery is God, Three in One. Here is the Christian's anchorage. The Father has chosen us; Jesus has shed his blood for us; the Spirit works in us to make us holy and lead us in obedience to Jesus.

JUNE 1

A Living Hope
1 Peter 1:3-9

Hope was at a premium in Peter's day. Biblical hope is never wishful thinking but an anchor of the soul. Here the apostle anchors his hope in two great past events. The first was the historic resurrection of Jesus of which he himself was an eyewitness. He had earlier preached that message with conviction in Acts 2:32. The second event was the re-birth of which verse 3 speaks. Peter could not preach the Easter message until he had known the Pentecost experience of Acts 2.

But hope is also assured in the future. There is in verse 4 an echo of the Old Testament picture of the promised land. Canaan often disappointed but heaven is absolutely secure. Not only is there a promised land, but there is a promised day to be revealed when our Lord himself returns (5, 7). Such hope can make the inevitable sufferings of life meaningful (6).

In the present, such a hope gives power for living. What we believe about the future inevitably affects the present. Verse 5 has a lovely balance. All comes 'by God's power' and is appropriated 'through faith'. Not only is heaven being secured for us, we are also being protected. All of this gives us the joy of which verse 8 speaks, even in uncertain days.

CuriousAngels
1 Peter 1:10-12

Most of us are vague in our knowledge of angels. But there is much in Scripture about them. Here Peter reminds us that angels peer into the gospel. The verb in verse 12b is that used of Peter himself and John when they peered into the empty tomb. Angels cannot know the wonder of the gospel message in their lives because they do not need the atoning work of Jesus. But they care deeply about the gospel.

What they see is a gospel planned from eternity and revealed even in the Old Testament. The prophets may not have fully understood the implications of their message. They would have been fascinated to hear Jesus' exposition on the walk to Emmaus where he points out the centrality of the sufferings of Christ in Old Testament teaching alongside the glory of resurrection life.

The angels also discover that the same Holy Spirit who inspired the prophets enabled apostles to preach that gospel and then enabled hearers to respond in faith.

We also know from the lips of Jesus himself that wherever lost sinners are found there is joy amongst the angels of heaven. Satisfying curious angels is yet another wonderful by-product of the response to the good news of Jesus.

Do You Mind?

1 Peter 1:13-16

Like his friend Paul, Peter follows clear teaching with challenging command. It does matter what we believe if we are going to behave in a right manner. For the rest of this letter Peter will be issuing orders which follow from the truths already studied. The immediate implication of believing in the hope is to live a holy life. So Peter in 2 Peter 3:14 will emphasise the same message.

Holiness is revealed in scripture as a characteristic of God, who is different from ourselves. Unique to biblical religion, holiness is not a ritual but a way of life. The Old Testament prophets were always thundering this home. It would be helpful to read Isaiah 1, Amos 5 or Jeremiah 7 to have this theme underlined. If we believe in a holy God then we must be concerned about holy living.

The marks of that holy living will be seen first of all in renewed minds which enable us not to be put off course by temptation. A renewed mind will lead to a controlled life. Then there is the call to willing obedience as children of our heavenly Father in verse 14. Such obedience inevitably means taking Bible reading seriously, discovering God's instructions in it and asking for grace to follow them faithfully.

JUNE 4

The Ransom Price
1 Peter 1:17-21

We have in our time rediscovered the whole concept of paying to redeem someone from captivity in the sad modern saga of hostages and their release. This is the language used by Peter as he illustrates the meaning of the cross. That was the supreme price paid to rescue people from sin and Satan. A released hostage understands how precious is that life into which he returns. So in verse 17 those who have been redeemed recognise that we now belong to the person who has rescued them.

The rest of this paragraph links with the thought of the Passover lamb whose blood was shed so that the children of Israel might come out of Egypt. Our own Communion Service, linked with the Passover meal, is a constant reminder of the centrality of the cross. Jesus in Mark 10:45 thought of it in terms of a ransom price.

The wonder of the cross is that it spans eternity and yet is very personal. It was not an afterthought by God but planned before the foundation of the world. Yet always in the New Testament there is a deeply individual element in it. It was for our sake that he died so that we might personally share his resurrection life.

Love Is The Badge
1 Peter 1:22-25

Some Christians love to wear badges. Ultimately Jesus insists that the real badge of Christian commitment is love. So Peter here sees love as the true demonstration of our new life in Jesus. But love is a very vague word.

Genuine love is seen as being 'sincere'. Peter also insists that this love should be from 'the heart', and that it should be 'deep', a word that literally means 'stretched out to the full'. It is easy to love those who love us and who are eminently loveable. The challenge of today's reading is to consider those whom we find it difficult to love and to pray for grace to do it.

Love is the supreme evidence of our new birth in Jesus which is seen in verses 23-25 as the work primarily of the Word of God. It is also manifestly the work of the Spirit of God, and these always work together. We are thus called to allow God's Word to work in our hearts and to believe that it is the power to work in other people's lives. When we allow the Spirit of God and the Word of God to work in our hearts we shall go on loving and be able to wear our badges with high confidence.

JUNE 6

Health Food
1 Peter 2:1-3

As with physical growth so with spiritual growth, there is a demand for regular discipline. First, we need to listen to Peter's negative command. Verse 1 lists some insidious sins with which we must deal decisively, if we are to lose our flabbiness as Christians and grow spiritually. There will be divine help in the process, but only we can deal with these hindrances to spiritual health.

Equally there is the positive challenge of verse 2. Children need right and regular feeding, so do Christian babies. It is a mark of children of God that they crave for food. They will start with 'pure spiritual milk'. The word 'spiritual' may be translated 'milk of the word'. It is through regular reading and study of the Scriptures that we grow.

No Christian should want to be a Peter Pan. We must be child-like but never childish. There must come a time when we will desire not just milk but meat. Read Hebrews 5:11-14.

Happily in verse 3 a good taste of God's Word whets the appetite for more. Not all health foods are appetising; but for the Christian the digested Word of God creates a longing for more.

JUNE 7

God's Building Project
1 Peter 2:4-8

Peter enjoys playing around with his own name. Jesus had given him the most unlikely new name of Peter, 'the rock man'. So here he assures Christians that they are called to become living stones built upon the foundation Stone which is Jesus. We must come to him alone, but when we come to him we are no longer alone.

These verses are full of Old Testament echoes around the theme of the building of the temple. The Christian church is a building of people on Christ, who was once rejected but is now the true foundation stone. Peter uses words which he heard Jesus use from Psalm 118.

Sadly, however, Jesus is not only the stone on which men build, he is also the stone over which people trip. You cannot be neutral with Jesus.

Alongside that picture is the Old Testament idea of Israel as the people of God called to be priests. So in verse 5 we see the Christian church is a priesthood. We do not have priests, we are priests; and the sacrifices we offer are no longer animals but living spiritual sacrifices. These include our bodies, our giving, our sharing with others and our praise and thanksgiving.

JUNE 8

The Church In Action
1 Peter 2:9-10

The church is not a building nor an institution but a people at work. Peter sees that church of which he was a foundation member as being a company of priests and prophets. Using language from Exodus 19 Peter reminds us that we are 'a chosen people, a royal priesthood, a holy nation, a people belonging to God'. We are this only by God's choosing. There was nothing special about the Jewish nation except that God specially loved them. So Christians belong to God and therefore become a priesthood. The priest is the bridge-builder. The church should build bridges between the world and the Lord, not least through our prayers.

But verse 9b demonstrates that our job is also to declare God's praises and especially as those who have come out of darkness into light. This is very much the prophetic voice. We are meant to be different and this must show in our life. But we are also meant to proclaim the gospel.

All this is only through God's grace. Verse 10 quotes from the prophet Hosea where God disowned his children as not really his own and then promised that he would bring them back. Our testimony is the grace of God that saves and keeps sinners like us.

JUNE 9

Into Battle
1 Peter 2:11-12

The Bible insists that there is always a battle in the Christian life. Sometimes this is an internal battle, and verse 11 is a loving warning from Peter that it will continue and often intensify. Therefore we must be careful not to give weapons to the enemy. We need to watch our sinful desires and keep them starved. Today the danger is that weapons are supplied to countries who want to wage war, and the people who supply the weapons are as guilty as those who use them. We must be careful not to give Satan an advantage.

Equally there is an external battle. As Christians we can expect to be misunderstood and persecuted. Jesus constantly reminded his disciples that they could not expect to have better treatment than he received.

But there is the great hope that the battle is not one-sided. We must not be always on the defensive. Verse 12 tells us that by good lives we may begin to win victories for Jesus. Peter's words here reflect those he heard in the Sermon on the Mount in Matthew 5:16. We must be concerned that our good works may bring glory to God and help in the battle.

New Look At Submission
1 Peter 2:13-17

One of the marks of the fullness of the Spirit in Ephesians 5:21 is submission; less exciting than the other great note of celebration but more powerful as a witness. So Peter insists that Christians should submit to every human institution, seen especially in relationship to state leadership. In verse 17 there are four commands given briefly and firmly. Remember that this command was to a group of people under the authoritarian rule of a Roman emperor. Jesus with his command to render to Caesar the things that are Caesar's and to God the things that are God's has a similar message. It is a reminder to pray for those for whom such submission can be painful.

All this is done 'for the Lord's sake'. Christian witness in every avenue of life is to be done as unto him. Only that motivation will enable us to keep going when the way is tough.

There are positive results from this biblical submission. Paradoxically it leads to real liberty (verse 16). Our world is desperately seeking to find this. Equally it helps to answer the slander of those who wish to destroy Christian witness. Consistent living may not make life easy but it does destroy empty criticism.

JUNE 11

New Look At Suffering
1 Peter 2:18-20

Christians do not have a monopoly of courage in the hour of suffering. What ought to be true is that Christians can go the second mile even when suffering is unjust as Peter indicates here. This is a situation where a believer should be able to do more than others in the terms Jesus used in the Sermon on the Mount.

These words are particularly challenging because they were written to slaves. We need to remember that over half of the population of Rome at this time would have technically been slaves, including people in very good positions. The New Testament does not encourage immediate emancipation. On the other hand it does not suggest that Christians should not protest against evil conditions. The supreme mark of a Christian slave is that he submits even when his master acts in a harsh way towards him. This is a demonstration of true Christian faith and love.

This is only possible when a slave is conscious of God (19). He needs to keep his eyes firmly fixed on him. Only when Jesus is central is this quality of living possible. It is one way in which a Christian, slave or not, can bear the marks of Jesus (Galatians 6:17).

Our A B C
1 Peter 2:21-25

Jesus is seen as our constant example. This word in verse 21 has the suggestion of perfect handwriting which we are called to copy. Supremely he was our example in the hour of suffering. The language of these verses echoes Isaiah 53. Even more it is Peter's own remembrance as he writes verse 23. He could not forget the insults, the crown of thorns, the mock king-making, the beatings and then the death of his Saviour on the cross. He was there, and he failed to follow.

But in the New Testament the cross is always much more than an example. In verse 24 we have a simple explanation of the atonement, very similar to Paul's language in 2 Corinthians 5:21. The death of Jesus was the only way in which we might be forgiven since he took our place. Not only Barabbas, but every sinner, can think of Jesus dying on his cross.

Only that way can a person return to the Shepherd and these tremendous verses indicate Jesus as both shepherd and sacrificial lamb. They also remind us that, on the day of Pentecost, Peter saw the cross as the result, not only of man's sin, but also of God's sovereign love (Acts 2:23).

JUNE 13

Ideal Home – Part 1
1 Peter 3:1-6

Models are vital in Christian witness. Model homes are all too rare. Church planting may well be less significant than home planting. So we will look at ideal homes with Peter in three instalments.

The longest section speaks of the responsibility of the wife in the home. In those days the Christian wife was much more likely to have had an unbelieving partner and therefore faced the greater challenge. As we evaluate this paragraph in the light of our contemporary situation we need to be sure of the positives.

Peter is not suggesting that to be submissive results in inferiority. He is not suggesting that wives should be silent agents. He is stressing rather the consistency of living. There is no encouragement to dowdiness in verse 3. Rather the emphasis is on an attractive character and a reminder of the danger of wrong perspectives.

We do not have the profile of a sweet and gentle lady only, but of one who is more concerned about pleasing God than men. The comment about Sarah should not suggest that this is old-fashioned. But there is a challenge to dare to go against the demands of contemporary culture in the concern to set up an ideal home of a biblical pattern.

JUNE 14

Ideal Home - Part 2
1 Peter 3:7

The challenge to husbands may be confined to one verse but it was revolutionary even to suggest that the husband too had a responsibility. Many men have doubts as to whether the wife is the 'weaker partner', but they do need to be challenged about being considerate and sensitive in their relationship. It is part of the radical change brought about by the gospel that men and women are seen as joint heirs, and this links with Paul's comment in Galatians 3:28 about there being no male nor female status in the kingdom of God.

In an age of constant complaints about sex discrimination, the church must be characterised neither by male chauvinism nor by female feminism. Rather the spirit of mutual respect and acceptance should prevail as a positive witness to a better way. From this verse comes a clear reminder that the spiritual life has precedence over every other aspect. Sexual relationships matter but our prayer life matters even more. Paul has some very wise words about this in 1 Corinthians 7:5-6. Nothing must hinder our walk with God which will have a value when the ideal home on earth is no more.

Ideal Home - Part 3
1 Peter 3:8-12

The church is meant to be a family, not only a family of families but a home for those who may have no earthly family. Churches need to be aware of the dominance of the family concept, and the danger of neglecting single people.

The church family should be characterised by harmony which is very different from unison, by feelings which go deep in sympathy and compassion, by a spirit of humility which follows the way of Jesus. With these qualities there will always be a home from home within the church.

The quotation from Psalm 34 is a reminder that God's protection and provision is promised for those who turn from evil, do good and actively seek peace. Here is the motivation for life at its fullest and days which are good in the biblical sense. There is however, as often, a warning even in the promise. The last phrase of verse 12 can be quite chilling with its reminder that God sets his face against those who spoil his purposes. We must be careful that we say and do nothing that would mar the family life of the people of God.

The Quiz
1 Peter 3:13-16

The quiz is a popular form of entertainment today. These verses remind us that a Christian will often be put on the spot in a situation more demanding than 'Mastermind'. We will be asked to give a reason for our hope. Often this will come with malicious slander (16) and in a context of fear (14). In scripture, faith is always the antidote to fear; these verses tell us how to keep faith alive when we are challenged.

Faith continues and does good whatever the situation. Whatever the false accusation, the Christian will not be swerved as he follows the example of his master. But there is a fear which remains. Faith has different things to fear. A Christian is more afraid of God's judgment than man's attack.

Because faith involves a complete commitment to the Lord, we always have an answer, but the answer must always be courteous. As we follow Paul when he appears on trial for his life in the Acts of the Apostles we see a man who would always turn the tables when he was accused, but always in a spirit of gracious love.

The Shadow Of The Cross
1 Peter 3:17-18a

Peter could never forget that the supreme example of suffering for good was in the death of Jesus. That was always close to his mind and conscience. He could vividly remember Jesus' trial, and how he failed his Lord in the hour of danger. So when Peter wishes to encourage his readers in their suffering he goes back to the cross. Jesus showed a complete commitment to God's will, and in the process of demonstrating that suffering love Peter goes back to the whole meaning of the atonement.

The more we believe about the significance of the cross the more it will challenge us to action. So verse 18a is crammed with practical theology. Jesus died for sins as a sacrifice; he died once for all, and nothing can change that act; he died as a sinless person in the place of others (2 Corinthians 5:21); he died to make the way back to God (John 14:6). In these statements lies the heart of Christian hope. Here too is the strength to keep going when we are called to take up our cross and follow him.

All The Way
1 Peter 3:18b-22

Here is complex, concentrated theology. But behind
it there is a picture of Jesus going all the way for us.
Between his death on the cross and the glorious resurrection of verse 22 he went to Hades on our behalf.
There he proclaimed his victory which has effect
across the whole of history. These verses do not
encourage us to believe in a second chance after death
if we have rejected the Saviour. But they do announce
that the cross overshadows everything and also that
Jesus went all the way through death for us. In him we
need not fear dying, any more than we fear death itself.

We too are called to follow all the way. Baptism is
primarily a pledge of God's saving grace and love. It
is illustrated by the story of Noah where a handful of
people were saved in the ark because they responded
to God's word. Baptism does not save us, but the cross
to which it always points does.

We too must make our pledge and go all the way in
response to him. Scripture always reminds us that
outward symbols are helpful, but they become dangerous if they take the place of reality. Read 1
Corinthians 10:1-13 and ponder.

JUNE 19

A New Chapter
1 Peter 4:1-4

The cross of Jesus is central to world history. Because of his physical and spiritual suffering we may have victory over sin. This is the promise for all those who are in Christ. Here is the turning-point both for world history and for our lives. Not only is the cross significant because we are in Christ; it is also a constant challenge to us to become more like Christ. The cross is both a place of atonement and an example. We too may expect to follow in the footsteps of Jesus, and therefore suffering should not be a surprise but an expectation. So Jesus promised in his Sermon on the Mount - the final beatitude in Matthew 5:11-12.

These verses remind us that suffering is often in the form of mockery and taunt which Jesus knew only too well. Because in our lives the old chapter is ended and a new one has begun, many non-Christian people feel threatened by the change, and therefore we, like Jesus, may know what it is to be taunted. This should never surprise us for it is one of the marks that we are bearing the cross of Jesus.

Once To Die, Then The Judgment
1 Peter 4:5-6

The words of Hebrews 9:27 help to make sense of these two difficult verses in Peter's epistle. In essence they remind us that however unfair life may be now there will be justice on the final day. That is why 'The Hallelujah Chorus' in the book of the Revelation comes at the fall of Babylon. Christians do not lightly rejoice in the downfall of anyone but there should be jubilation at the final conquest of sin and the end of injustice.

That final day will be double-edged. The Old Testament ends in Malachi 4 with this theme and Paul speaks clearly about it in 2 Thessalonians 1. The judgment will be by our Lord himself, as he comments in John 5:27 and Paul underlines in Acts 17:31. Whether dead or alive on that day we shall stand before Jesus, and those who have rejected him will face the awesome reality of the wrath of the Lamb.

These verses remind us that eternal life begins not on judgment day but on the day we face up to the claims of Jesus. Then we begin to live in the Spirit. Significantly the word for life in verse 2 speaks only of biological life, the word in verse 6 implies eternal life.

JUNE 21

Living In The End Times
1 Peter 4:7-9

For the Christian the last days are always round the corner. The New Testament ends with that conviction in Revelation 22:20. Jesus encourages us to live each day as if it were the last. In one sense the end times, in which we are living, began with Jesus' first coming (1:20). Aware of this fact, we should not get excited but live consistently and in a state of readiness.

This will involve three priorities. In the first place there is the priority of the mind. We are exhorted not to be fools but to make mature decisions. The rich farmer who was not prepared for eternity was not condemned as wicked but as foolish. Then we are told to have prayer as a priority: prayer for ourselves and our worthiness and prayer for the world to turn to Christ while there is still time. The final priority is that of love and Peter speaks of it with great passion. He remembers the Lord telling him to forgive continually which is always a mark of love. In a practical sense love shows generous hospitality.

A person who believes the end is round the corner is the most attractive person in the world.

Stewardship
1 Peter 4:10-11

Stewardship is an important biblical word and is used here in verse 10. It implies responsibility for the use of our money - very much needed today. But it also speaks of God giving particular gifts to correspond to the need. The verse also speaks of 'God's grace in its various forms'. This adjective has been used in chapter 1:6 as 'all kinds'. God has his answer to every need and we are meant to be part of that answer. Every gift is of God's grace and therefore should be used for the good of the whole and never for personal gratification.

Two gifts are especially mentioned. They are equally important. The first is speaking, which must be in line with biblical truth so that we know we are speaking God's very words. The second is service, which is needed just as much in the life of the church. All Christian servants need to be filled with the Spirit as were the deacons in Acts 6 of whom two, Stephen and Philip, became great preachers. Servants can become speakers. But all must be done to God's glory, and Peter pronounces a doxology even before the letter ends.

No Surprises
1 Peter 4:12-14

We may assume that Peter had news when writing this letter, since in verse 12 persecution appears to be imminent, whereas in chapter 3:14 it had seemed vague. Whatever the truth, he is now very tender in his teaching about suffering for the sake of Jesus.

His main argument is that we should never be surprised when this is our lot. We should not be surprised because our Lord promised it in Matthew 5:11-12. We should not be surprised because Christians do pose a threat to the world when living consistently. We should not be surprised because suffering has a purpose in our lives. And, not least, we should not be surprised because it draws us closer to our Lord and his sufferings.

Peter, who has learned his lesson intimately, can call Christians to rejoice as he and the other disciples did in Acts 5:41 when they shared the sufferings of Christ.

Suffering brings a person nearer to Jesus and assures him of the hope of glory.

The Family Name
1 Peter 4:14-16

Surprisingly, the word 'Christian' rarely occurs in the New Testament. Verse 16 is one of the occasions as is Acts 11:26 and 26:28. The nickname, given at Antioch was, often an occasion for stigma and suffering. When Christians name children in baptism or dedication they pray that they will not be ashamed to confess the name of Jesus. Christians should bear the name of Christ unashamedly (14). The New Testament speaks of power in that name in Acts 3:16. It also speaks of suffering in that name in John 15:21.

Those who bear the Christian name should be consistent. There is always the danger of deserved persecution due to bad Christian living. Verse 15 challenges us not least by the last word 'meddler' which is unique in the New Testament. It speaks of being busybodies, poking our nose into other people's affairs unnecessarily. That kind of person deserves persecution.

But if we honestly suffer because of our nickname, we are reminded in verse 14 that it is the pathway to true happiness and glory. Let us be sure that we are not ashamed of him and even more that he is not ashamed of us.

Judgment Day
1 Peter 4:17-19

The Bible speaks of judgement, rather than charity, beginning at home. It is a common biblical theme that God will expect much of those who bear his name and to this end he purifies his church. In the Old Testament God speaks of judgment beginning at the sanctuary and, through his prophets, he condemns those priests who had forgotten their high calling. At such an hour of testing it is easy for a child of God to lose heart. Job kept his head (Job 1:21) but sadly his wife sought to swerve him from his constancy (Job 2:9-10).

If we are tempted to betray our Lord when suffering, these verses remind us that judgment upon those who disobey God's gospel is infinitely greater with its eternal consequences, cf 2 Thessalonians 1:8-10.

The exhortation to put their confidence in the faithful Creator (19) should encourage God's people. If we believe that God is working everything for good to those who love him then we can happily trust his will. In Gethsemane, Jesus put God's will first, not in passive resignation but in willing acceptance. After this commitment we are then freed from fear to get on with the job of doing good while there is time.

JUNE 26

What's In A Name?

1 Peter 5:1-4

These verses contain three titles for Christian ministry: elders, pastors and bishops or overseers. To the Christian minister titles should be of no importance, but they do indicate a work to be done. Peter recollected that Jesus had called him to be a shepherd in that breakfast interview with the risen Lord in John 21. Jesus told Peter to prove his love for him by caring for his people - feed my sheep. He also remembered his master's words about the good shepherd in John 10 and how Jesus embodied that pastoral care.

Christians should be characterised not by titles but by the spirit of their service. It should be willing, not under duress, eager to serve, not greedy for gain; self-giving and not self-seeking. Our example is our Lord who knows his sheep by name and laid down his life for them.

Our lives are constantly being tested by God, and one day the quality of our service will be revealed when we meet the Chief Shepherd. There will be a reward of which we need not be ashamed. It is a spiritual reward which will make all the hard work of pastoral care infinitely worthwhile.

JUNE 27

The Sign Of The Towel
1 Peter 5:5-7

I know of someone who keeps a towel in his study to remind him of his ministry. That has a good precedent. Jesus demonstrated the life of service by clothing himself with a towel, and Peter remembers it vividly because he was intimately and embarrassingly involved in the incident. Verse 5 echoes this occasion as Peter talks about clothing ourselves with humility.

This exhortation applies especially to young people who, by virtue of their life and enthusiasm, are most important in the church, but who must learn from older people. It is a call for all who follow Jesus and who do not wish to find themselves being opposed by a God who hates the proud.

Often we strive in our own strength because we are anxious about the future. The real antidote for anxiety is humility, for all too often self-importance and a fear of hurt pride, underlie our anxiety. Verse 7 applies to those who take the towel. If we believe the second half of that verse with its gospel assurance of the Lord's care for us, then we can easily throw our cares upon such a Saviour.

Spiritual Warfare
1 Peter 5:8-11

Peter is still in reminiscent mood. He remembers vividly the words of Jesus in Gethsemane when he had failed to keep awake and pray. Our Lord had counselled him to watch and pray, aware of the weakness of the flesh. He had said similar words to him in Luke 22:31-32 about Satan's subtle activity. Now Peter passes on the message to others.

We are instructed to know our enemy. Satan comes in different guises, like a lion, as here, or sometimes masquerading as an angel of light (2 Corinthians 11:13-14).

But equally we are to remember that we do have resources to fight him. Some of these resources lie in ourselves. We are to tap these resources by being alert, and by resisting the devil, assured that others are in the same fight with us. United we stand. But supremely our resources are in our God who will allow suffering and even use it to strengthen his people. Ultimately he who calls us will see us through to the end. All the verbs in verse 10 suggest stability. The word 'restore' is the word for 'mending nets' which Peter well understood. In Christ we will be strong, firm and steadfast.

JUNE 29

Greetings
1 Peter 5:12-14

The eastern world spends time greeting people. In the West, we tend to be perfunctory in our greetings. At the end of his letter, Peter gives a lovely glimpse of the fond greetings of other believers. Silas his secretary, to whom can probably be attributed the good Greek of this letter, sends a message. John Mark, gloriously restored after lapses in the past, is now called 'my son Mark'. Read the end of Acts 15 and realise what a wonderful reconciliation this means. The whole church sends its greetings (probably the church in Babylon is another name for the church in Rome). Here is a cameo of Christian fellowship so vital in the fight against evil.

The final word of the apostle himself is one of love and peace to encourage Christians to stand fast. As Peter remembers what has been written in this letter to believers under persecution, he reminds them that it has been a letter of both encouragement and testimony. Here is the balance of all Christian ministry. We proclaim the truth, and in the strength of it encourage others to keep the faith. Loving fellowship without biblical content can easily evaporate. Solid truth without love is far removed from the Lord who is full of grace and truth.

JULY

MAURINE MURCHISON

The God We Worship

God Is Omniscient

'O LORD, you have searched me and you know me' (Psalm 139:1).

Our minutes and days are links in the chain of life forged together by the absorbing concerns of daily living. We look downwards, consumed with care by earthbound anxieties. To take time with Psalm 139 is to change perspective. Troubles become trivial and self unimportant when we are faced with the reality of an omniscient God.

Psalm 139, written by David, is a record of his personal relationship with God. He begins by speaking to God as 'LORD', as his own God, as the covenant God of Israel.

This prayer is disturbing. It is not too hard to pray if we imagine we prevent God's searching eye from coming close. But how difficult it is to say, 'O Lord, you have searched me and you know me'! The God of the universe is concerned with every aspect of my life and being. He knows me intimately - God, the mighty Creator whose dwelling is in the heavens, knows me better than I know myself.

'Everything is uncovered and laid bare before the eyes of him to whom we must give account' (Hebrews 4:13).

God Knows

'You know when I sit and when I rise; you perceive my thoughts from afar' (Psalm 139:2).

Grandchildren bring back double memories - memories of our own childhood and memories of our children's early years. As a little one cuddles down in her cot it seems comfortable once again to repeat the bedtime prayer: 'Lord, protect me through the night, and keep me safe till morning light'. Centuries ago, David prayed using a similar thought, that God knows both our waking and our sleeping movements. We may be active, all consciousness of God banished from our minds, or resting, unaware of God's care for us. Yet he is aware and is concerned with our every step and every activity of our outward lives.

But there is something more wonderful than this. God knows our inward lives as much as he knows our outward ones. The intentions of our hearts are understood by God. There is no motive, no thought concealed from others and often barely admitted to ourselves, which is unknown to our Lord. We may deceive ourselves, but we cannot deceive him. We may conceal our sin but it is known to him.

God's care for the believer is such that every detail of his existence is encompassed by infinite divine knowledge.

JULY 2

God Sees

'You discern my going out and my lying down; you are familiar with all my ways' (Psalm 139:3).

As I sit in my study, I can hear a car bumping over a metal grid. There is no need for me to go outside to know what's happening. My neighbour has left early to shop. Some things, however, I don't know: I don't know when she plans to return, I don't know who she'll meet and though I know a little about her habits I am certainly not 'familiar with her ways'.

This psalm tells us that there is someone who does see all that we do. There is no part of David's lifestyle with which the Lord is not acquainted. The pattern of his life is clear and open before God whether in its monotonous regularity or its haphazard variety. The Lord saw his daily routine as he led his sheep out on to the Judaean hillside. The Lord watched him as he lay down beside still waters, as he fled from King Saul and as he lazed in his palace, distracted by the sight of beautiful Bathsheba. Everything that David did was open and familiar to his Maker.

'You are the God who sees me' (Genesis 16:13). Would we change the pattern of our lives if we really understood that the Lord is 'familiar with all our ways'?

JULY 3

God Perceives Thought

'Before a word is on my tongue you know it completely, O LORD' (Psalm 139:4).

Our children were used to having grandparents living under the same roof for most of their early childhood. It proved to be an excellent training for me as a mother. When I disciplined the family I had to discipline myself. I would have been ashamed for my parents to witness uncontrolled anger and so I rarely lost my temper.

There are times when we can control the words 'on our tongues' before we speak them but there are other times when we don't even know what we are going to say. The words flow from our mouths - words of anger and hurt, or words of wisdom and grace. Yet what we say reveals what we secretly think, and what we think reflects what is in our hearts. We may try to impress others but from God we can conceal nothing; he perceives us for what we really are.

May our speech reflect the grace of God in our hearts. 'May the words of my mouth and the meditation of my heart be pleasing in your sight, O LORD, my Rock and my Redeemer' (Psalm 19:14).

JULY 4

God Encloses

'You hem me in - behind and before; you have laid your hand upon me' (Psalm 139:5).

The butterfly was becoming exhausted. It was the wrong side of the glass and beating against the window in a vain effort to reach freedom. I trapped it, carefully putting my hand over the fluttering wings. Once outside, I opened my hands and it sailed upwards, the red sheen of its wings catching the sunlight.

David had a similar experience of God. Everywhere he turned, God was there. If he went forward, God was present; if he retreated, God was blocking his path. David was truly 'hemmed in'; there was no escape. All around him was God's presence cornering him.

Yet there was more than that. 'You have laid your hand upon me,' David writes. The picture is of the open palm of the Almighty being placed over the believer, holding him in his power. Not only is God omnipresent, he is also in total control. While his hand may prevent us from wilfully going our own way, it will also protect us from harm. It encloses us only to do us good.

Jesus said, speaking about his own, 'No one can snatch them out of my hand' (John 10:28).

JULY 5

A Wonderful God

'Such knowledge is too wonderful for me, too lofty for me to attain' (Psalm 139:6).

I mostly missed out on science in school and have never caught up on the subject since. To me the operation of machinery, the workings of a computer and even domestic equipment are quite incomprehensible. Yet I recognise that others have used their education, extended it, researched further and understood. Such knowledge is impressive, but at least I can trace its progress. It is remarkable but within the capability of the human mind.

The knowledge of which David writes is of a different order: it is supernatural, limitless and all-knowing. This is knowledge distinct from the human, divine in its essence. It is the capacity to know the totality of all that has happened, is happening and will happen in the universe; the capacity to understand all the processes of creation and nature, and yet focus on one believer and know more about his thoughts and actions than he does himself.

Do we approach this God with a due sense of wonder or are we superficial in our dealings with him? 'Surely I spoke of things I did not understand, things too wonderful for me to know' (Job 42:3).

JULY 6

God Watches

'Where can I go from your Spirit? Where can I flee from your presence?' (Psalm 139:7).

I was four years old and had refused to eat up my porridge. Grandmother had found my plate and was looking for me. Crouching in the angle between two walls, I pressed myself against the hard stone as if somehow it could cover me. Very soon she came, an old lady in black, waving a stick and calling my name. She put out her hand and drew me back to obedience. The reality was that she loved me and I could have ended our disagreement if I had run back to her and confessed.

David, conscious of his sin, asked whether it was possible to escape from a holy and all-knowing Lord. He discovered, as I did when a child, that our hiding-places do not conceal us. There is no place where God's Spirit is not present and where we are not watched by the penetrating eye of God. It is foolish to imagine that since we cannot see God, he cannot see us.

To escape from God's righteous anger we must turn towards him in repentance and faith.

JULY 7

God Of The Universe

'If I go up to the heavens, you are there; if I make my bed in the depths, you are there' (Psalm 139:8).

Beneath the wings of the aeroplane lay barren golden mountains, devoid of plants, their peaks topped with snow. The Andes stretched below us, an alien landscape too high and infertile for man or beast. Even in that inhospitable terrain, God was present, as he was in the heavens around us.

David could only imagine what it might be like to rise into the sky above Palestine - over the mountaintops - and beyond that to heaven itself. Perhaps, he thought, up there he could escape from God, or even in the opposite direction, down to the depths, the world of the departed spirits. But his conscience is clear - even there God is in control.

'In heaven he shines with beams of love,
With wrath in hell beneath;
'Tis on his earth I stand or move
And 'tis his air I breathe' (Isaac Watts).

'The heavens, even the highest heaven, cannot contain you' (1 Kings 8:27). God is present in the highest heaven and the lowest hell. In one he blesses his own, in the other he judges the lost.

JULY 8

God Holds Fast

'If I rise on the wings of the dawn, if I settle on the far side of the sea, even there your hand will guide me, your right hand will hold me fast' (Psalm 139:9,10).

The setting was a hospital in Belgium, the patient our daughter having her first child. My privilege was to support her with my right hand, my arm encircling her head as she reached the end of the labour. My presence was there to reassure her, to hold her fast in her exhaustion and to rejoice once her little one was born.

A note of similar reassurance has come into Psalm 139. David would have watched the sun rising over the Judaean hills and sinking over the Mediterranean sea conscious that God was there from east to west. Unexpectedly the Psalmist's understanding has changed - no longer fleeing from God he now takes strength from his presence. 'Even there', at the uttermost parts of the known world, God's hand is present - not to punish or chastise but to guide and to hold.

'For I am the LORD, your God, who takes hold of your right hand and says to you, Do not fear; I will help you' (Isaiah 41:13).

JULY 9

God Lights

'If I say, "Surely the darkness will hide me and the light become night around me," even the darkness will not be dark to you; the night will shine like the day, for darkness is as light to you' (Psalm 139:11,12).

Total darkness is frighteningly oppressive. Only once was I down a coal-mine and the most alarming part of the experience was when the lights in our helmets were all put out. I stood for two minutes in blackness so complete that I imagined it pressing in on me physically. In that dark pit surely a man could hide without fear of detection.

Yet David discovered otherwise. Even in darkness he cannot escape the presence of God - the all-seeing One. For God is himself light and needs no earthly light to guide him. The darkness itself turns into light for God and the night shines as day.

'Light of the world! Undimming and unsetting,
O shine each mist away!
Banish the fear, the falsehood and the fretting;
Be our unchanging day' (Horatius Bonar).

'The city does not need the sun or the moon to shine on it, for the glory of God gives it light, and the Lamb is its lamp' (Revelation 21:23).

JULY 10

God Creates

'For you created my inmost being; you knit me together in my mother's womb' (Psalm 139:13).

The psalmist has understood that God knows all about him - what he is doing, what he is thinking, and that there is nowhere in the whole universe where he can escape from God's presence. But beyond these awesome truths is another full of blessing and wonder: God's knowledge was rooted in his activity as creator of David's very body as it was being formed.

Today we can see the shape of a little body moving on a monitor screen when a pregnant mother has a scan to check her baby. I watched the four tiny chambers of a grandchild's heart as they contracted regularly. The little one was only sixteen weeks into its life in the womb, and yet parts of the body were clearly visible. David had never seen a foetus moving within a mother yet he was able to say with confidence that God's hand had been at work as he developed months before his birth.

God has cared for us from the first instant of our conception. He has watched over us and created us with his purpose in view for each of our lives.

God's Works Are Wonderful

'I praise you because I am fearfully and wonderfully made; your works are wonderful, I know that full well' (Psalm 139:14).

It was 1951 and the village we visited was in west Holland. It was no ordinary community. Each house sheltered a group of mentally-handicapped people, some acutely deformed and others apparently normal. We saw helpless children and strong young men, some bedridden, some active. My abiding memory was of one young man, exceptionally musical and yet in all other respects like a small child.

It's easy to complain about our own minor deficiencies, blemishes of form or character inherited from birth. We forget that we all, handicapped or otherwise, still retain elements of the image of God. Like David, we can each praise God because he has made us as we are, in a way that is fearful, since our lives are so fragile and wonderful, in the intricacy of the body and its relationship with the soul. And we can demonstrate praise by using the body he has given us in his service.

'Fill thou my life, O Lord my God,
In every part with praise,
That my whole being may proclaim
Thy being and thy ways' (Horatius Bonar).

JULY 12

God's Artistry

'My frame was not hidden from you when I was made in the secret place. When I was woven together in the depths of the earth, your eyes saw my unformed body' (Psalm 139:15-16a).

The Belgian nurse asked our daughter as she waited in the delivery-room, 'Do you know if it's a boy or girl?' She replied that she didn't want to know until the baby was born. 'But we know, we have seen,' said the midwife. Next morning when baby Kate was tucked up in a pink-lined basinette prepared before the birth, her mother understood the significance of the coloured sheets already set out for her.

David's mother had no modern tests to tell her about her unborn baby. Yet David knew that although he was hidden and unseen in his mother's womb (the 'depths of the earth') till the moment of birth, he was not hidden from God. God was there at his beginning, both seeing and creating. 'Our bodily frame is like a very skilful piece of embroidery, curiously wrought; its nerves, veins and muscles are fashioned with divine art' (Charles H Spurgeon).

A God who takes such interest in our creation can be trusted with the detail of our lives.

JULY 13

God Writes

'All the days ordained for me were written in your book before one of them came to be' (Psalm 139:16).

God has a book and in that book he writes the names of his people. David here emphasises a glorious truth - that not just his name but the whole of his life is recorded by God, day by day, and those days were recorded and planned even before they happened. This is the highest point of David's understanding of the all-knowing, ever-present God. The God who knows his innermost thoughts and created him, who saw him within the womb, had outlined the pattern of his life even before he was born. The glory is God's, the comfort is the believer's. If God knows the end from the beginning, why should the believer worry about the future?

'Set free from present sorrow,
    We cheerfully can say,
E'en let the unknown morrow
    Bring with it what it may -
It can bring with it nothing
    But he will bear us through;
Who gives the lilies clothing
    Will clothe his people too' *(William Cowper)*.

JULY 14

God Cares

'How precious to me are your thoughts, O God! How vast is the sum of them! Were I to count them, they would outnumber the grains of sand.' (Psalm 139:17-18).

The room could have looked very bare - lino-tiles on the floor, plain walls and functional fittings. The bleakness was broken by colourful cards and baskets of flowers, reminders from friends and family that they cared and thought of me as I faced the future in that hospital room. I rejoiced in their love and wondered that they had taken time to show it. I drew closer to them as I experienced their loving concern.

And so, in a much more wonderful way, David drew near to God as he began to contemplate God's care for him. God knew him intimately, thought about him lovingly, and ordered matters for David's good. It was no wonder the psalmist was awestruck when he considered that Almighty God cared so much that his thoughts about his servant were more numerous than the sand (an example used in the Bible to speak of something that cannot be counted).

'Cast all your anxiety on him because he cares for you' (1 Peter 5:7).

God Is Faithful

'When I awake, I am still with you' (Psalm 139:18).

Little Beth was restless. She curled up in her cot half asleep, disturbed by the slightest noise. I stroked her forehead but when I lifted my hand, she stirred again. Her mother was out and she sensed her absence. There was some security in knowing Granny was there when she opened her eyes but what she really needed was to see her mother beside her when she woke.

The pattern is the same for the believer. Often we go to rest anxious and unaware of the presence of God, carrying our troubles into sleep and waking unrefreshed. David understood that the reality was otherwise. God never leaves us as a human parent must. The God whom David needed had not gone away. On the contrary, God was still with him and in control of all his circumstances. Like David we may sleep with confidence in the power and care of the omniscient God. Our first waking thought should be that we are still with God - the night has not separated us from him.

'I will lie down and sleep in peace, for you alone, O Lord, make me dwell in safety' (Psalm 4;8).

JULY 16

God Judges

'If only you would slay the wicked, O God! Away from me, you bloodthirsty men! They speak of you with evil intent; your adversaries misuse your name' (Psalm 139:19-20).

We are either friends of God or enemies of God. David recognised this distinction. He had become aware of how awesome was God's searching of his life and soul, how comforting was the constant presence of his Lord. In contrast, there were those who hated his Lord, who spoke evil of him and misused his name to achieve their own wicked plans. David wanted nothing to do with those who opposed God's holy purposes. They must either turn from their evil ways or perish.

The language of these verses sounds harsh in this age of unlimited tolerance, but when we pray in the Lord's prayer 'Your kingdom come', we too are asking for the destruction of Satan's realm and of the enemies of God just as David did in this petition.

'Chosen to be soldiers, in an alien land,
Chosen, called and faithful for our Captain's band.
In the service royal let us not grow old,
Let us be right loyal, noble, true and bold' *(F R Havergal).*

JULY 17

God Expects Loyalty

'Do I not hate those who hate you, O Lord, and abhor those who rise up against you? I have nothing but hatred for them; I count them my enemies' (Psalm 139:21-22).

David had experienced loyalty. Jonathan, son of King Saul and David's closest friend, had supported him in spite of the implacable hatred of the king. And after Jonathan's death, David, hunted like an animal in the hills, had been followed by a group of brave men. Three of them had risked death just to bring their leader a drink of water from the well in Bethlehem, where their enemy the Philistines had their garrison. That was the kind of loyalty which David understood a holy God demanded of him.

God's followers must show their colours, stand up and be counted. The Christian is eternally indebted to Christ for salvation and we reveal our understanding of that indebtedness by being prepared to stand beside our Lord and to align ourselves against evil.

'I'm not ashamed to own my Lord
Or to defend his cause;
Maintain the honour of his Word,
The glory of his cross' *(Isaac Watts)*.

God Searches

'Search me, O God, and know my heart; test me
and know my anxious thoughts' (Psalm 139:23).

I have memories of London during the Blitz; memories of bomb dust, of barrage balloons and bright
beams of light piercing the blackness of the night sky
over a city condemned to darkness. The searchlights
were both fearful and comforting; fearful lest they
discovered the enemy plane or missile with its potential for destruction, and comforting since they revealed the attacker for the anti-aircraft guns to shoot
down.

David began this psalm by acknowledging that God
had searched him. As he contemplated what that meant,
he understood something of the all-knowing, ever-
present and all-powerful God. The knowledge was
fearful - he could not escape from the searchlight of
God's knowledge - and yet comforting - in the hands
of such a God he was protected. So he ends the psalm
by asking God to search him exhaustively.

When a believer prays to be searched by the living
God, it is not because he thinks he is without sin but
because he knows his hidden sins are such that only
the presence and power of God can deal with them.

JULY 19

God Examines

'See if there is any offensive way in me, and lead me in the way everlasting' (Psalm 139:24).

Sometimes we need to suffer an exhaustive search even when it may be painful. If I have a tooth filled, I am anxious that every particle of decay is drilled out, so that I do not lose the whole tooth. I do not expect my dentist to leave a doubtful spot just because it would hurt me to have it removed. The searching probes must clean out all the offensive corners.

So it was with David and his innermost being. He asked God to probe, to examine, to root out any corrupt inclinations. He does not put off the process, or cover up the rot, but is prepared for the examination, painful though it might be. For a hidden root might develop into open sin and offend the holy God whose comforting presence surrounds him.

'Think and be careful what you are within,
For there is sin in the desire of sin;
Think and be thankful, in a different case,
For there is grace in the desire of grace' *(John Byrom)*.

JULY 20

God Answers

'Out of the depths I cry to you, O LORD' (Psalm 130:1).

It was the middle of the night. Our six-year-old son lay sobbing in his bedroom, acutely ill with encephalitis. I was so distressed that I left him with his father, shut myself off from the sound and cried to the Lord from the depths of anxiety. And in handing him back to the Lord my anxiety gave way to peace.

Most of us will have had our 'depths' of personal suffering, intolerable stress or the 'dark night of the soul'. At such times we may turn to God, unable to pull ourselves from the depths, but looking upwards to the only one who is able to reach down and bring us out, to set our feet in a firm place and rescue us from despair.

For the psalmist, his intense need seemed to be for mercy and forgiveness rather than rescue from immediate circumstances. Our greatest need is also a spiritual one, and if our hearts are aware of the depth of that need we will cry out to God to bring us up out of sin into pardon and peace.

'Before they call I will answer; while they are still speaking I will hear' (Isaiah 65:24).

JULY 21

God Listens

'O Lord, hear my voice. Let your ears be attentive to my cry for mercy' (Psalm 130:2).

Mothers seem to be in a constant state of alert. To the outsider there seems little difference in the baby sounds coming from a crowded crèche but a mother will pick out her own child's cry immediately. As a mother I reacted at once when I heard any one of the family call out for me. There was a subconscious awareness of their dependency and years after the youngest was no longer a baby, I would turn round when I heard a child cry in case it was one of our own.

That listening sensitivity of a parent is what the psalmist is seeking in this prayer. He is in intense need, in critical danger, and he calls out to the Lord asking him to listen to his prayer even from the depths of doubt and backsliding. Sometimes all we are able to do is to ask for mercy and we can find no more words to express our troubles. Spurgeon suggests: 'When we have already prayed over our troubles, it is as well to pray over our prayers'.

'If we ask anything according to his will, he [God] hears us' (1 John 5:14).

JULY 22

God Records

'If you, O LORD, kept a record of sins, O Lord, who could stand?' (Psalm 130:3)

One new school policy is to maintain a 'record of achievement' for older pupils so that when they leave school they can take with them a detailed report of what they have achieved during their school career. These records aim to encourage and praise rather than blame and condemn.

God too keeps a record. He keeps a record of our sin and, as the psalmist realised, if that record were to be used in judgment, he could not stand innocent before God. The list would include sins of omission and sins of thought and action. There would be no successes or achievements untainted by sin in that book, only failure and transgression. But for the psalmist there is an 'if'. For him, the Lord forgives and does not condemn since he stands not in his own righteousness but in that of his Saviour.

God Forgives

'But with you there is forgiveness; therefore you are feared' (Psalm 130:4).

One of the most rewarding experiences of childhood is when a little one, banished for disobedience and wrongdoing, runs back to his parent's arms. He knows that when he 'says sorry' there will be forgiveness and love which wipes out all the anger. At that moment, the child, repentant and restored to favour, respects his parent and only wants to be obedient rather than suffer the torment of being cut off from love.

The psalmist expresses the same feeling here. God's nature is to be merciful, to pardon and forgive, and he has provided a way back to himself for the repentant sinner through the sacrifice of Jesus Christ. The after-effects of this forgiveness are that we 'fear God' - in other words, we have a desire to obey him, a longing not to grieve him, or to risk losing his presence in any way. Our fear is no longer of condemnation but of losing a consciousness of God's favour and grace.

If we, like children, come to him confessing and forsaking our sin, 'he is faithful and just and will forgive us our sins and purify us from all unrighteousness' (1 John 1:9).

God Is Faithful

'I wait for the LORD, my soul waits, and in his word I put my hope. My soul waits for the Lord more than the watchmen wait for the morning' (Psalm 130:5-6).

My husband and I waited in a dirty, sticky apology for an airport. For six hours we sat among children selling peeled coconuts, and soldiers vigilant against terrorists. Our waiting was in vain as the plane, already full, flew over the jungle town without landing.

The psalmist's waiting was different. He waited for someone who would not disappoint him. There was only anticipation, for God had promised and it was safe to put his hope in God's word. As the watchmen guarding the city knew for certain that dawn would break after the black night, so the psalmist knew his God would surely come. As they longed intensely for the relief of daylight, so the psalmist longed for the joy of meeting with his Lord.

'Great is thy faithfulness, O God my Father.
    There is no shadow of turning with thee;
Thou changest not, thy compassions they fail not;
    As thou hast been thou for ever wilt be'
                                    (Thomas Chisholm).

JULY 25

God Is Merciful

'O Israel, put your hope in the LORD, for with the LORD is unfailing love and with him is full redemption. He himself will redeem Israel from all their sins' (Psalm 130:7-8).

This psalm begins in the depths of sin and despair and ends in the heights, confidently extolling God's mercy and love. God has come as he promised, and come with an unfailing love that befriends and an unlimited power to redeem. His redemption is full (or 'plenteous') and embraces all sins. It does not just deal with the punishment of sin but includes forgiveness. It breaks the power and dominion of sin in the heart and life of the believer and sets him free from the consequences of transgression.

However deeply the believer may be caught in the pit of sin, there is a way out to a firm place of confidence. The cry for mercy from the place of repentance brings the psalmist to the rock of assurance where he can wait for a forgiving God, rejoicing in the fullness of a merciful redemption.

'Here is mercy that receives sinners, mercy that restores backsliders, mercy that keeps believers... Mercy is like God, it is infinite and eternal. Mercy is always on the throne' (James Smith).

JULY 26

God The Shepherd

'The LORD is my shepherd, I shall not be in want'
(Psalm 23:1).

The first thing that I can remember is standing on a table as a two- or three-year-old in a bright upstairs room, while my father held me firmly as he taught me some verses. Those verses have stayed with me all my life - the well-known words of Psalm 23 in the Scottish metrical version. The 'shepherd psalm' has become familiar to many people; they sing it at school, at weddings, and at funerals. Words that are familiar are somehow comforting. They make us feel sentimental, secure.

But sometimes the secure and comfortable can be dangerous. We may rest in those words without really thinking what they mean, without realising that they demand a commitment, a personal faith. David was writing about a Lord whom he knew, whom he called 'my' shepherd. As the sheep he himself had tended trusted him to look after their needs, so he knew that he could trust God to care for him. But like the sheep, that care depended on his belonging to the shepherd.

Jesus said, 'I am the good shepherd; I know my sheep and my sheep know me' (John 10:14).

God Leads

'He makes me lie down in green pastures, he leads me beside quiet waters, he restores my soul. He guides me in paths of righteousness for his name's sake' (Psalm 23:2-3).

One very wet, windy day, my husband and I huddled together watching a shepherd guiding his sheep. He was not in a grassy field gathering them with dogs, but on a Mediterranean hillside, stepping carefully along narrow tracks as the sheep followed him. Some stupid ones got into awkward corners, some foolhardy ones perched on the cliff-edge, and the stragglers got left behind and went their own way.

There are those in this life who do not want to go God's way; the paths of righteousness seem too narrow, or too hard or too steep. They think it more interesting to go their own way, on easier, more pleasant paths. But for David it was enough to follow his Lord, who knew where to find the still waters where his soul would be restored. One definition of a Christian is someone who follows Jesus. It is not enough to claim to know God if we do not follow him.

'My sheep listen to my voice; I know them, and they follow me' (John 10:27).

JULY 28

God Comforts

'Even though I walk through the valley of the shadow of death, I will fear no evil, for you are with me; your rod and your staff, they comfort me' (Psalm 23:4).

Some years ago, I was reaching the end of a long tunnel of fear. I had had major surgery for cancer, and chemotherapy afterwards. The night before the operation, part of me was afraid; afraid of what the doctors would do to me, afraid of what they might tell me, afraid of what they might be hiding from me. Then the words of this verse came to mind as I lay waiting for morning to come; they were comforting words that assured me I was not alone in that valley of the shadow and they turned my fear into peace.

David knew that he would have to walk through the valley of the shadow of death at some time in his life; nor did he deny the reality of fear. But he knew the antidote to that fear, the presence of his Lord to comfort him.

'Be with me when no other friend
The mystery of my heart can share:
And be thou known, when fears transcend,
By thy best name of Comforter' *(A H Vine)*.

JULY 29

God Provides

'You prepare a table before me in the presence of my enemies. You anoint my head with oil; my cup over-flows' (Psalm 23:5).

During the war years, if the warning siren sounded, our school class had to escape to the brick shelters and stay there until the end of the raid. Sometimes we had to eat there - a scant meal of emergency rations kept ready for the purpose. We were, in a sense, having a meal in the presence of our enemies.

David, too, was provided for in the presence of his enemies, who attacked him from within and without all his life. Yet this was no minimal ration but a feast where he was an honoured guest at a banquet. His head was anointed with perfumed oil, and his cup overflowed with drink. He followed a generous master who provided not the minimum but much more than he expected. The Lord's spiritual gifts - an abundance of peace and joy - were far beyond what David deserved.

However difficult a believer's circumstances may be, he or she can taste of God's provision so abundantly that contentment and grace will overflow to benefit those around.

'The blessing of the LORD brings wealth, and he adds no trouble to it' (Proverbs 10:22).

JULY 30

At Home With God

'Surely goodness and love will follow me all the days of my life, and I will dwell in the house of the LORD for ever' (Psalm 23:6).

At the end of a day on the hillside, as the sun set, the sheep came to rest in the fold. They had been surrounded by the shepherd's care all day. He had seen that they had had enough food and chances to rest, that they were protected from enemies and that if they strayed they were brought back. Weary with their travelling, they could now rest in peace and safety in the fold, with their shepherd sleeping across the door to ensure that they were not harmed.

David understood that as the sheep had a home awaiting them, so had he. On the road of life he was attended by goodness and love. Goodness supplied his needs and love blotted out his sins. And finally content to reach home, he would find his Lord already there. Unlike the sheep, he would have no more days of wandering and danger. His Shepherd's house was his eternal home, a place of rest and joy in fellowship with the Lord.

'Now the dwelling of God is with men, and he will live with them. They will be his people, and God himself will be with them and be their God' (Revelation 21:3).

JULY 31

AUGUST

ROBERT AMESS

*The Love
of God*

A Church Divided
1 John

When a local church splits for reasons other than growth, people get hurt. This sad event, so prevalent today, affects everyone, leaders and people alike. The outcome is discord and bitterness. Healing is invariably protracted and painful. Into just such a situation, John writes his first epistle.

A cursory glance reveals that 1 John is unlike a usual epistle. There is no address at the beginning, nor are there any personal greetings at the end. Neither, for that matter, can I detect any structure of the material in between! Now that illustrates what invariably happens when a church splits - normal conventions, courtesies and structures go out of the window!

Comparison with John's Gospel makes it clear that the author is the same. Here is that quality of simple language and profound thought. Many of the recurring themes are the same - 'light', 'love', 'truth', 'faith', and the centrality of the person of Christ. The writer is the aged John of Ephesus, who himself, decades before, had been the beloved disciple of Jesus. No wonder the note of maturity and parental concern that John displays to his confused readers!

The Life Revealed
1 John 1:1-2

Never forget that ours is a revealed faith. We are not Christians because it feels good. John, in his epistle, writes of what he has heard, seen and handled. What he has heard is truth, what he has seen is the demonstration of the power of God, what he has touched is the Word of life made flesh. Here is an eye-witness to the incarnation.

The key phrase of the epistle is 'that you may know'. And what is that? Firstly, certain facts concerning the incarnate Christ, and, secondly, certain great benefits he came to secure. 'We proclaim to you eternal life'.

One would imagine that John would at once set out to tackle the problems in the church. Not at all. What he does is to establish the theological foundations from which he will eventually apply his teaching and counsel. He is an Apostle of Christ. He has seen the Lord, and has been commissioned by Christ to establish and pastor the church.

That is the basis of his ministry. First, the foundation truths, and then addressing the problem. That is still the essential method for meeting today's needs.

AUGUST 2

The Life Proclaimed
1 John 1:3-4

All preaching must be for a purpose. Unless we can ask, 'What difference has it made?' then a sermon has been a waste of time for both preacher and hearer. As with John, there must be a 'so that' in all proclamation.

After setting down his foundation, John at once enters into his purpose for writing, and it is twofold. Firstly, that the broken church to which he writes might experience restored fellowship, and, secondly, that their fellowship with the Godhead might lead to complete joy.

For those who have experienced a common salvation there must be a common life. That's fellowship. To know eternal life is to have fellowship with God, and then, inevitably, fellowship with the family of God. True fellowship is 'the coming together of the children of God in a common service of love for Christ's sake'. The ignoring and denial of this fundamental truth is as much a sin today as it was when John wrote to this divided church.

The inevitable outworking of this fellowship is joy. There is something wrong with a Christian life that does not smile or sing. Complete joy is being one with the Godhead and one with each other.

AUGUST 3

Light And Darkness
1 John 1:5-7

No one can describe God. He is greater than any definition man could give. Yet in his sovereign purpose God has revealed certain things about himself. John gives us a positive and a negative. 'God is light; in him there is no darkness at all'.

Light is shorthand for all that God is. It speaks of him as Creator, for 'Let there be light!' were the first words of creation; omniscient, for light is knowledge; sinless, for light is pure; omnipotent, for it has been discovered that pure, concentrated laser light is very powerful. In the light of God there is nothing that obscures, deflects or spoils - no darkness at all. John did not come to this knowledge himself, it was given to him by revelation.

And what has this revelation to do with us? The whole epistle will give the answer. As always, it must have practical consequences. If we claim to have fellowship with the light, our lives will bear the scrutiny of the light. Unless we are liars our lives will confirm our claims. We will have fellowship with the children of the light, and the ongoing cleansing power of the blood of Christ will keep us clean.

AUGUST 4

The Sin Problem
1 John 1:8-10

Wouldn't it be wonderful to be sinless! No more battles with evil, complete victory over temptation. To claim such a thing is a deception, says John bluntly. Light always casts shadows. To deny the shadow of sin in our lives is simply to deny the truth. In fact, it is to make God out to be a liar. To claim sinlessness is either to have a deficient understanding of God, or to have an exaggerated and defective view of ourselves.

Though not often preached today, the erroneous doctrine of sinless perfection seems to be widely implied. Let me explain. So few seem to mourn the fact of indwelling sin. Few appear to feel the pain of sin's power. The pride of some seems almost to imply sinlessness.

For those of us who know we are sinners, and lament the fact, then our passage contains one of the key verses of the Bible. True confession must be personal, springing from the heart, and particular, dealing with issues and failures. And how can I know that my sin has been forgiven? By confession, through the finished work of Christ, and because God is faithful and does what he has promised.

AUGUST 5

Never Be Blasé About Sin
1 John 2:1-2

Unlike the original writers of the epistles, the people who inserted the chapters and verses into the Bible were not infallible! These verses follow on immediately from what went before.

With paternal graciousness, John brings these vital truths to his readers. Permission is never granted for a Christian to sin. Any particular sin in the believer is not inevitable, nor is it regarded with tolerance. So the text does not say 'when' but 'if' anyone sins. A holy person is not one who cannot sin, but one who is resolved not to sin by the grace of God. Nevertheless, in the light of the perfection of Christ, all of us feel condemned.

That is why the scene moves to the court-room of heaven. Here is our Advocate; the original is *Paraclete*, the one who stands by our side to represent us - a comforter. The four other times John uses the word, it refers to the Holy Spirit; but here he is speaking of Christ himself.

Our Advocate is the Lord Jesus. Being himself righteous he is qualified to represent us. And what is the ground of his appeal? He pleads himself, the world's only Saviour, the sacrifice for our sin.

Knowing God
1 John 2:3-6

'That you may know' is one of the major themes of the epistle. At a time when conflicting claims were being made by leaders of this church, the ordinary member needed to know who was speaking the truth.

Here is a man who says, 'I know him'. Then we have the right to ask of this man, 'How is your knowledge worked out in practice? What difference does it make?' Three times in the first chapter John has said, 'if we claim', then certain things must follow. Our claims must be supported by the way we live.

In his epistle, John brings three tests to bear upon our claims. We have the first of them here - the test of obedience. To know God is to obey his commands. Here are the grounds of assurance: we desire to walk as Jesus did. Knowledge, for John, is never just an intellectual thing; it is moral and spiritual, worked out experimentally and motivated by love. Jesus said, 'If you love me, you will obey what I command.'

Mark the progression in these verses from 'to know him', to 'living in him'. That is real knowledge: communion with God, knowing something of the walk of Christ.

The Test Of Love
1 John 2:7-11

Here is the second of the three tests I referred to yesterday. Love is such a cardinal matter to John that he returns to it again and again. In these few verses so many of John's key words are brought together: truth, darkness, light, love and hate. He is teaching about absolutes. John speaks of a new command. At once I imagine John's readers were put on their guard. They had heard enough new things lately! But there was no need to worry. This new command is an expansion of the oldest and greatest commandment - Deuteronomy 6:5, and quoted by Jesus himself.

John seems confused: is this command new or not? Jesus, speaking of love, says, 'as I have loved you'. That is new. There has never been love like this before. This old command is to be newly applied in the light of Christ's love. Like two sides of a coin, love to God and love to man, each is essential to the other. If God is my Father, then his children are my brothers and sisters in Christ. If I love Jesus, then I must love those he loves and died for.

An Important Digression
1 John 2:12-14

Some preachers are so well prepared that they never digress. That's a shame, because, as with John here, it's so often then that they are at their most interesting. John speaks to believers at different points in their spiritual growth. Why do so many Christians stay as spiritual infants for so long? Perhaps the answer is in the child's explanation for falling out of bed, 'I went to sleep too near where I got in.' Why do so many grow old, cold? Now, if only I had an explanation for that! God's purpose for the normal Christian life is spiritual progress and growth to the day we die. That is a constant New Testament theme.

John uses two words for children: *tekna* at the beginning of the chapter are the ones to whom he writes, and *pidia*, meaning literally, 'children', or in this context, 'spiritual babes'.

So John says to all believers, 'Your sins have been forgiven'. To children, 'You have known the Father'. Young people receive the most attention: they understand, are spiritually strong, and are on the victory side. Fathers know more and more of God, and, by implication, have a responsibility for the young men and children. What a vital and ignored ministry for today!

AUGUST 9

Do Not Love The World
1 John 2:15-17

As a student I had a vacation job on the wrong side of London Bridge. Let me explain. Twice a day I walked in the opposite direction from what seemed to be the whole of London walking the other way to or from the city. A Christian often feels like that. Everyone else seems to be busily making for somewhere different from us.

John uses the word 'world' in many different ways. Sometimes the world is God's creation, and, despite the fall, there is still much to enjoy there. Then the world is the object of God's redemptive purposes: 'God so loved the world'. Into this world we are told to go with the gospel - the good news.

Here, the 'world' is synonymous with the 'god of this world', the devil. This fallen, immoral, material-istic world hates Christ, and therefore hates us. This world of which John speaks is concerned with its own advancement, and is rooted in time rather than eter-nity. Love for the world is love that shuts out love for the Father. This is not just negativism. Be positive, seek to do the will of the Father, live as children of eternity. Say, with Paul, that 'for me to live is Christ'.

The Test Of Doctrine
1 John 2:18-19

In God's timescale this is the last hour. The mark of that is the activity of many antichrists. For teaching on the antichrist we have to look at Thessalonians. How are we to recognise the antichrists of which John speaks? They deny that Jesus is the Christ.

The test of everyone is their relation to the Lord Jesus Christ. One of the marks of Christian maturity is the ability to disagree in love on secondary issues. But if anyone denies the person and work of Christ, however persuasive his argument, that one is an antichrist, and we must stand against him. Jesus warned that deceivers would come, and they are a feature of every age. This is the never-changing test: 'What do you think of Christ?'

Inevitably the application of this test causes division. Here is an issue over which we must divide. If 'they' had not left us, we would have had to leave them. A church split caused by a matter of no fundamental importance denies the prayer of Christ 'that they may be one'. But to be equivocal about who Christ is, is to be in league with the antichrists, and to fail the test of doctrine.

The Anointing
1 John 2:20-23

How can I be sure that I am of the truth? The answer is given here: 'You have an anointing from the Holy One'. The Greek word for 'anointing' is *chrisma,* which is not to be confused with a similar word *charismata. Chrisma* speaks of the Old Testament anointing with oil. Gradually the word was applied to the anointed one - the Messiah of God. The Greek for Messiah is *Christos* - Christ, the Anointed One. At Antioch the disciples were first called Christians, or followers of the Anointed One, or even 'the anointed ones', those who had received the promised Holy Spirit.

This was the experience of those to whom John writes: 'You have an anointing'. 'It's not from me,' says John, 'but from the Holy One, and its outworking is truth.' It could not be otherwise, because Jesus had promised, 'He shall lead you into all truth'. Christians are never led into error by the Holy Spirit.

Here is the cardinal test. This is how you can know the truth. The anointing reveals Christ: who he is and what he has done. Anyone who denies that is a liar and an antichrist. Whatever else his claim, he knows neither the Father nor the Son.

Remaining In Christ
1 John 2:24-27

The anointing which we described yesterday is not just that we may discern who Christ is, but also that we may remain in him. We sense that John is reminded of the teaching of his Master in John 15.

This is a complex age. Even in evangelicalism so many conflicting voices are saying, 'Follow me.' 'Come to this conference.' 'Read this book.' 'Hear this preacher.' 'Respond to this new teaching.' All of us know something of these pressures.

Where is the truth to be found? John seems to infer that the one who remains in Christ has an inner sense of truth. 'You do not need anyone to teach you' does not mean that there is no need to be instructed in the faith - far from it. These people had already been well taught. And what was the nub of that teaching? It was the need to remain in Christ. For when we remain in Christ, he has said, 'his words remain in us'. We know the truth.

That is why John speaks of eternal life here. 'This is eternal life:' said Christ, 'that they may know you, the only true God, and Jesus Christ, whom you have sent.'

Confident And Unashamed
1 John 2:28-29

John has been speaking of the believer's privilege. Because of the anointing for the children of God, there is specific teaching concerning 'all things' that we need to know. Now the responsibility to remain in Christ is amplified. 'Continue in him, so that when he appears...'

The fact of the Second Coming of Christ is attested to by nearly every New Testament writer, and by the Saviour himself. The word 'appear' means more than just seeing Christ. The Revised Version translates it 'when he comes as clear light'. As the children of darkness we would have dreaded the light of Christ, but for the children of God there is an unashamed confidence.

As the Prodigal Son was brought home with a robe around him and shoes on his feet, so can we say with John Wesley's translation of Zinzendorf,

Jesus, Thy blood and righteousness
My beauty are, my glorious dress.

But, once again, these things are not to be presumed upon. There is always Christian responsibility. Continue in him, do what is right, so that when he comes we shall be confident and unashamed.

AUGUST 14

We Shall See Him As He Is
1 John 3:1-3

Here is a high-water mark of revelation. John is speaking of great love. Not our love, but the Father's love lavished upon us. Love's beginning is with the Father, who is love. Love's object is 'us', you and me in Christ. Love's achievement is that we should be called 'children of God', with all that that implies. To be a child speaks of access to the Father, care, direction and provision for all our needs. Of these things the world is totally ignorant.

John moves from our present position in the family of God to describe our future experience. There is no doubt that Christ is coming again. There are details over which we may differ; but this we know: we shall see him. And, what is more, 'we shall be like him'. Now that is almost too wonderful to take in! The sight of Christ will be ravishing - beyond description. It will be transforming because it will have to be! It will be eternal, never coming to an end.

Once again John applies these things practically to our present situation. Everyone who has this glorious hope of the coming of the Lord keeps himself clean.

AUGUST 15

Habitual Sin
1 John 3:4-6

The disruptive leaders who had wrought such havoc in the church not only claimed to be sinless, they implied that they could live as they liked. For them, external, so-called peripheral things, did not affect their basic sinless standing with God. The technical name for this heresy is Antinomianism. These verses have been the subject of much controversy, but taken in context they are painfully clear.

Sin is breaking the law of God, and is opposed to the gospel of Christ, who took our sins away. Therefore, anyone who is in Christ will never delight in, or condone, sin, or habitually sin on purpose. There is no teaching here to support either sinless perfection, or the possibility of losing one's salvation. John has already said that if we claim to be without sin then we are liars.

So what is the explanation? Just this: when a Christian sins, for that moment he does not live in Christ. In fact, he behaves as if he were a fallen man. Trespass is walking on someone else's property - the devil's. People who continue to sin on purpose, and are untroubled by it, should ask themselves whether they are truly in Christ.

AUGUST 16

Facing The Facts
1 John 3:7-10

When believers sin they contradict the mission of Christ. Sin is of the devil, and the Son of God came 'to destroy the devil's work'. In these verses, John speaks with a father's love, yet with a father's firmness. On these fundamental matters of the faith do not let anyone lead you astray. Sin is of the devil and foreign to the life in Christ. Sadly, Christians may fall into an error of judgment. They may be overtaken by temptation, or be contrary to the will of God, but they will not live as enemies of God. Sin is deadly serious.

Now which sin would we use to illustrate this truth and apply it to our experience? Adultery perhaps? Or pride, or greed, or temper? Preferably something to which we do not feel prone ourselves. But John uses an amazing illustration - the failure to love one's brother. How strange! But think a moment. The sinning life is the selfish life. It is a rationalisation of the things that suit us. It is a denial of Christ. 'This is my commandment, that you love one another.'

We live in continual spiritual warfare against darkness. We might lose a battle, but Christ has won the ultimate victory.

AUGUST 17

Loving One Another
1 John 3:11-15

Everything we know of John confirms the centrality of love, both in his experience and expression. Having been loved much, he radiates love constantly.

Today we begin a new section of the epistle, yet John's constant theme is unchanging, and, as ever, is absolutely practical. 'I found your message very moving,' a lady said to a preacher. 'Where did it move you?' came the rather caustic reply. We must constantly insist that the things that we hold and firmly believe make a practical difference, both personally and corporately. Sadly, love for our brothers and sisters does not seem to be the distinguishing mark of modern evangelicalism. Here is the truth declared by John: 'We should love one another.'

Surely John goes over the top in using Cain and Abel as an illustration? I've never murdered anyone! 'Anyone who hates his brother is a murderer,' says the scripture of truth.

The hatred of the world toward us is to be anticipated, but hatred in the church is never to be tolerated. In fact, one of the grounds for assurance, the way we can know that we have passed from death to life, is the love we have for the family of God.

AUGUST 18

How We Can Know What Love Is?
1 John 3:16-20

I would be the last to despise doctrine. Right foundations are essential for the guarding and building of the church. But the Christian life is more than doctrine. Christ's love for us was practical and cost him everything. He laid down his life for us. In the light of that sacrifice 'we ought...' Ought has a note of constraint linked to reluctance about it. The things 'I ought' to do never seem to register high on my list of priorities. Yet, if we do not show the love of Christ, who will?

John tells us a story. Here is a man who has material or financial need. Here is another who has the wherewithal to help, and sees his brother's situation. Yet he does nothing to help him. He ignores his need. How can the love of God be in him?

There is a clear echo here of the parable Jesus told in Matthew of the sheep and goats. 'Whatever you did for one of the least of these brothers of mine, you did for me.' The ones sent into eternal punishment were accused of no sin at all, save that they were without practical love.

AUGUST 19

Confidence To Ask
1 John 3:21-24

A clear conscience leads to a freed tongue. If I know that the matters that spoiled my relationship with God have been dealt with and removed, then I can come to him, unburden myself, explain freely what is on my heart and mind and ask him for anything. Because of the walk of obedience, the fellowship is close and the dialogue frank and free. Our Father is not reluctant to give, and is certainly able to meet all that I need.

Perhaps it sounds just a little too easy. But note that there is a guard here. This promise is restricted to the one who pleases God, who does what he commands. If we do things that are pleasing to him, we shall ask for things that are pleasing to him. And, as always, remember the context. The motivation for our asking is not ourselves but others, and the 'I' will begin to become less prominent in our prayers. The context is love for the brethren.

So it is that John gives us a twofold command. To believe in the name of God's Son and to love one another. Believing and living the gospel of Christ through the Spirit he gives.

Test The Spirits
1 John 4:1-3

So many today claim an intimate knowledge of the will of God. One of the dangerous trends of the age is the tendency to say 'The Spirit told me', or 'I was led of the Lord'. Of course it puts someone beyond the possibility of debate. No one would want to argue with the Lord. The prophets referred to in the passage speak not only of those who exercise the gift of prophecy, but also of any teacher in the Lord's name. 'Do not believe every spirit', is John's injunction.

Deuteronomy requires two tests of prophets. If what they say is not true, or if what they say is true but leads people away to other gods, then they are to be put to death. Now if that sounds rather drastic you will understand what an important matter we are addressing here.

John adds another test. What is the prophet's understanding of, and relationship to, Christ? The responsibility to apply this test rests with every Christian. John says two things. Firstly, be careful, for there is the spirit of antichrist in the world. Secondly, apply the test. Does this exalt Christ and build up his body the church? If not, resist it. Have nothing to do with it.

On The Victory Side
1 John 4:4-6

Here is vital teaching that seems to be largely forgotten. With the emphasis on spiritual warfare, the power of the devil, the reality of demon oppression, etc., many have forgotten that 'the one who is in you is greater than the one who is in the world'. The theme is still false prophets. Never forget that Satan is mighty, but there is a mightier. The strong man has been defeated by a stronger. By the work of Christ on the cross, the evil one has been dethroned and Christ has been enthroned.

> Should all the hosts of death,
> And powers of hell unknown,
> Put their most dreadful forms
> Of rage or malice on,
> I shall be safe; for Christ displays
> Superior power and guardian grace.
> *(Isaac Watts)*

Neither is this battle for truth fought alone. We are from God, and not from the world, and God is with us and in us. In this conflicting age, with its many strident voices, we can know what is false by the Spirit of truth who has been given to us.

The Demonstration Of God's Love
1 John 4:7-12

It's all very well John constantly telling me to love people, but does anyone love me? God is the source and origin of love. He is love. Prick me and I bleed, prick God and he loves. Love is the very essence of God. Love is not just one of the things that God does; all his activity is loving activity.

It needs two to love. If a man were never to meet another human being he would never understand what love is. There might be a sense of longing and unfulfilment, but not love. This is one of the proofs of the Trinity. Even before the creation of the world, or the creation of the angels, God was never alone. 'In the beginning was the Word.' There has always been love in heaven. God did not love the world because he created it. He created the world because he is love. Love must be demonstrated. That is the meaning of the 'providence' of God. It is the care of God for all that he has made. Yet the love of God is more than providence; it is grace. This is how God showed his love: he gave his only Son.

Blessed Assurance
1 John 4:13-16

All this seems rather similar to what has gone before, namely the love of God. The basic meaning here is, that being possessors of the Holy Spirit, we know, experience, enjoy and radiate the love of God. Understand that the Holy Spirit is given freely. He is as much a free gift as God's free gift of his Son. From this it follows that he is given without measure or qualification. Any limitation is by us and is our responsibility. By the indwelling Spirit we know the Father and the Son who is our Saviour.

Fourteen times John tells us 'that you may know'. These verses are Trinitarian. The blessed assurance of which John speaks is ours through the work and ministry of Father, Son and Holy Spirit. Here is the definition of true happiness. God living in us, and we living in love. Love expresses itself. It cannot but reveal itself. Living in love must be the happiest thing in the world.

If someone says, 'I love you', we have the right to reply, 'Show me that you love me'. God has demonstrated his love towards us. The spontaneous demonstration of our love shows that we live in God.

AUGUST 24

Perfect Love Drives Out Fear
1 John 4:17-18

Paul tells us that love never ends (1 Corinthians 13). John assures us that there is no fear in love. Therefore I can look forward to the day of judgment with perfect confidence. What a dreadful day that will be for many! But for those who are ready for his appearing it will be a day of peace through the love of God. 'O love that will not let me go!'

Let's look at this word 'confidence' a little more closely. It does not mean bravado or arrogance. That day will be so solemn as to be contemplated with awe and godly reverence. But there must be no dread in it. If there is awe, it is because of the occasion, not because we are frightened of the verdict. Look at the face of the Judge - he's your friend. In his love we are safe for eternity. By his love we are like him - in his Son. By grace he sees me as in his Son who has died, and is satisfied.

Fear is a horrible thing, with so many dreadful repercussions, both spiritual and physical. Fear has to do with punishment, and demonstrates to me that I am not perfect in love.

AUGUST 25

He First Loved Us
1 John 4:19-21

God is not cold, hard or unemotional. Nothing could be further from the truth. He is love. And this is the wonder: not that he loves, but that he loves us. Perhaps for the pure, brave and upright we could imagine a degree of affection. But that God should love the fallen, sinful people that we are is pure grace. God demonstrates his own love for us in this: while we were still sinners, Christ died for us. The love of God precedes our love, and is the source of all our love.

Yet again John grounds these truths in the reality of our daily experience. What he seems to be saying is this: 'If you do not love your brother whom you can see, which is easier, how can you love God whom you have not seen, which is harder?' Ah, but you don't know my brother! The word that John uses is not *philos* - human love - but *agape* - God's love. It does not mean that I must like my brother; I must love him as God loved me. Not a sentimental or merely sympathetic love, but a self-sacrificing, self-denying love. This agape love is very costly.

Victory Over The World
1 John 5:1-5

'Our faith' is 'believing that Jesus is the Son of God'. And it is this same Lord Jesus who by his death and resurrection has won the victory, and overcome the world and the god of this world. There is power in the name - the only name given amongst men whereby we must be saved. So our faith is a mighty living force. We 'can do all things through Christ who strengthens us'. Or again, 'we are strong in the Lord and the strength of his might'. Without Christ, life is hopeless. Only by his power can we be on the victory side. This is not to be an intellectual understanding, but a present experience. A living and loving relationship with the living and loving Lord.

That is why the carrying out of his commands is not burdensome. Christ's yoke is easy and his burden is light. One of the lies of the devil is to imply that the will of God is hard, and the walk of faith unattractive. It has been said, 'God is no man's debtor'. To follow hard after the Lord is to know 'life, and health, and peace, and everlasting love.'

AUGUST 27

The Spirit's Testimony Of The Son
1 John 5:6-12

There is little doubt that verses 7 and 8 are a later interpolation. They are found in none of the trusted Greek manuscripts. That does not mean that the doctrine of the Trinity is in doubt. This essential truth is in the testimony of all the scripture.

Here is vital teaching concerning Jesus Christ. He is the Son of God, the promised Messiah. He has been born a man - 'You are to give him the name Jesus, because he will save his people from their sins.' He has publicly stood in the sinner's place and died as a sacrifice for sin. The completion of this great work was sealed by his resurrection and ascension into heaven. The gift of the promised Holy Spirit is the proof that, having received all power in heaven and on earth, he now reigns head over all. This is the testimony of God concerning his Son, which we believe and have in our hearts. All who believe in the Son have eternal life. This testimony to the heart is a priceless gift by the Spirit.

God's Holy Spirit with mine doth agree,
Constantly witnessing, Jesus loves me.

AUGUST 28

Drawing Together The Threads
1 John 5:13-15

Some things we need to be told again and again. In these verses John ensures that certain fundamental truths have been understood and applied by his hearers. It will do us no harm to make sure that we have grasped them also.

Every believer can know that he has eternal life. This is the clear declaration of the Word of God. Not to appreciate or appropriate that, hinders joy, dishonours God, cripples witness, and certainly interferes with our spiritual growth.

What are the marks of those who by the grace of God and the finished work of Christ have trusted in him for their salvation? Assurance and faith; a desire to live the godly life; a real tangible love for the family of God; the inner witness of the Spirit; true joy; a discernment as to the truth. All these things John has been speaking about at length. And, oh yes, don't forget, a confidence in approaching God in petitionary prayer. Our confidence comes from knowing that God buries our mistakes in prayer. He gives us what we would most desire, if we could see as he sees. The apparent limitation is our freedom in prayer.

AUGUST 29

Real Prayer
1 John 5:16-17

If we truly believe that prayer changes things then we will get down to real intercession. Neither will our prayers be taken up with the trivialities of much of that which is called prayer today.

It must be accepted that these verses are difficult. There would seem to be support here for the Roman Catholic doctrine of venal and mortal sin. That is not so. The brother to whom John refers seems to be a similar case to the one to whom Paul refers in Galatians. 'Brothers, if someone is caught in a sin, you who are spiritual should restore him gently.' John says, 'Make it a matter of real, believing prayer.' And what are we to pray for? That 'God will give life'.

And what about the 'sin that leads to death'? John does not actually forbid us to pray. From the standpoint of our finite minds we are never in a position to count any condition hopeless. Can a mother not pray for her child, or a wife for her unconverted husband? Such a thing would be as outrageous as it is impossible. Paul implied, 'If Christ saved me he can save anyone'. Pray on, trust the God who gives life.

AUGUST 30

God Keeps Us Safe
1 John 5:18-21

John is so sure and confident. In this epistle there has been no hesitation or doubt. He has spoken with a quiet confidence and full conviction. Here, three times, he tells us that we can be confident too. Here he speaks of our divine origin, 'born of God', of our abhorrence of sin, and our defence against the evil one.

Right to the end, John glorifies Christ; Jesus, the One with whom he walked and talked along the dusty Galilean roads. That same Jesus is the true God, and eternal life.

What is our relationship to Christ? Do we know the things of which John has been speaking to be true? Have we been born of God? Do we know God?

We must not imagine that there is now nothing else to learn, that we know it all. God has so many more things to teach us from his Word. God grant that skimming through this great epistle has whetted our appetite to know yet more of the things of God and his Christ. Paul, right at the end of his ministry, said, 'That I might know him'.

And, of course, one last practical exhortation: 'Dear children, keep yourselves from idols.'

SEPTEMBER

REBECCA MANLEY PIPPERT

With God
In The
Wilderness

Hannah: 'Everyone Is Someone To God'

1 Samuel 1:1-20

The book of Samuel comes at a time in Israel's history when the Philistines were pressing in upon them, there was to be a transition from theocracy to monarchy, and Israel's very existence was becoming critical. Within this crisis the book opens not with a battle or a dissertation on the need for leadership, but with a private family problem. Elkanah's two wives had a long-standing quarrel. Hannah turns to God in desperation, praying and promising to dedicate her son to God if he will remove the disgrace of her barrenness. That one prayer resulted in Samuel - a man who grew into one of the greatest leaders Israel had ever had.

The God of all creation cares, not only for the affairs of state, but for the 'small things' concerning individuals. Never be ashamed to bring your requests to God. In his great economy, God's answer to even the most intensely personal prayer may be used to benefit a nation. Pray boldly for the small things. Remember that the nation of Israel was changed for ever by the prayer of one woman who dared to believe that the infinite resources and powers of God were at his disposal to work on behalf of his people.

SEPTEMBER 1

Pain That Leads To God

1 Samuel 1:21-28

Human hearts are not only sinful but wounded. Our wounded areas can be the catalyst that turns us to God, or they can give birth to bitterness and self-pity. The power of Hannah's story is not that she got exactly what her wounded heart cried out for - but that she had the freedom to give back to God the very thing she thought she could not live without. To allow anything other than God to be what defines or gives us worth is not only a recipe for disaster but is the breeding-place of idolatry.

Hannah's wholeness did not come from Samuel; her peace came before she was even pregnant. More painful than her barrenness was her sense that God had forgotten her. What transformed her life was her realisation that God was directly involved in her life and loved her. She could give Samuel back to God because now he represented not her worth, but God's; the God who had 'remembered' her. Once we know that truth by heart, our idols and enemies lose their power over us. Our wounds become a blessing if we allow them to lead us to God.

God - The Parent We Can Trust
1 Samuel 2

What parent does not long to protect his or her child from the harsh realities of life? Hannah not only sacrificed raising Samuel, but she allowed him to be brought up in a Temple that was fast becoming notorious for the sinful practices of Eli's sons. Imagine Hannah's feelings as she heard stories of Temple life! No doubt her prayers deepened as her faith was tested. The worst form of evil is when the sacred and the obscene are united. Witnessing pagan debauchery is far less damaging than seeing contemptuous religious hypocrisy. Objectively, one would think Samuel stood a much better chance being raised by his own loving godly family than where he was.

This environment could have produced a bitter man who felt abandoned by his parents, and spiritually cynical. Instead, we find a thoroughly wholesome boy who was never corrupted by the ungodly behaviour around him. Why? Above all, it is a testimony to the keeping power of God. God called Samuel, and he could be counted on to protect Samuel. God takes seriously the commitment of children to his service. We can entrust our children to God, who will parent them with the same skill and devotion with which he has parented us.

SEPTEMBER 3

Even Evil Is Not Wasted
1 Samuel 2

Children are shaped by the godly example of their parents. Samuel saw, even if only once a year, his mother's selfless devotion in contrast to the self-indulgence of the priests. And he no doubt heard from Eli about the power of her prayers!

But we live on a fallen planet that is subject to evil. To think we can protect our children from seeing this is folly. Samuel's training about sin was learned at the Temple, which surely shows us that no place is free from sin's reach. What gives us hope is that God can use even the examples of sin to train our children. Just as Samuel's family modelled the importance of obedience to God, so Eli's sons revealed the inevitable and disastrous consequences of sinful choices. Samuel saw what rebellion against God looked like at close range, which enabled him to discern Saul's rebellion almost from its inception.

Samuel had to learn to recognise God's ways and resist temptation in an evil world. So must our children. But our confidence is that God will waste nothing in building the kingdom of God in our children - even evil!

God's Call - Our Choice

1 Samuel 3:1-4:1

What made Samuel such an extraordinary leader is rooted in three things. First, he was called and chosen by God to be a leader. Second, God used his cultural environment to train him in leadership skills. Thirdly, he made godly choices. We see this in his response to the Lord's calling. When God called Samuel he got up three times in the early morning to respond to what he thought was Eli's call. That says much for his character and self-discipline. It was his willing obedience that enabled God to use him mightily.

As important as calling and culture are, it is the choices we make that reveal whether we are submitted in obedience to the command of God. Obedience to God's word was the prerequisite for Samuel being used and finding favour with God. It was the test that would bring Saul down and cause David to succeed. So will it be for us. We either stand for the Lord and repent and conform to his truth, or we stand alone and suffer the consequences.

SEPTEMBER 5

Following God's Best Plan
1 Samuel 9,10,12

The leaders of Israel asked Samuel to appoint a king so they could be like the other nations. God did not want them to be like other nations. But Israel persisted in its demand for a king in spite of the Lord's warning. God granted their request and established Saul as king, with the condition that Israel was to consider the Lord as its ultimate ruler. But even after the great victory at Jabesh-Gilead, Samuel reminded the people that their desire for a king to lead them instead of God was sin. He explained that God was graciously blessing them in spite of their wrong choice, not because of it.

What a comfort it is to know that God has mercy on us in our shortcomings! He will take a bad request made with bad motives and use it for his own purposes. Nonetheless, think what we sacrifice when, because of our rebellion, we must take God's redemptive second best. As C S Lewis says, 'Whatever you do, he will make good of it. But not the good he had prepared for you if you had obeyed him. That is lost for ever.' How much better to obey the Lord and receive the first best that he desired!

SEPTEMBER 6

Do Not Forget the Lord Thy God
1 Samuel 9, 10, 12

God chose Saul to be the first king, and he supernaturally confirmed his decision to Saul through a series of fulfilling prophecies. When God directed the people to Saul he was found hiding in some baggage. Although modest, Saul seemed to be a choice young man in the prime of life. He was physically attractive and most of the people were delighted with their new king. Their delight turned to ecstasy when Saul succeeded in destroying the Ammonite forces. What was the key to his success? 'The Spirit of God came upon him in power.'

God chose Saul, he made him king, and he empowered him to do the task. The only condition to experiencing God's favour was simple: love and obey the Lord and never forget who is in charge. If we honour the Lord, the Lord will honour us. How simple, and yet how easily we forget! Success seduces us into believing that what we have comes from our own hands and not the tender mercies of God. To be human is to have a 'God-complex' which readily credits self for success, and remembers God only in difficulty. God wants to lead us into the land of milk and honey. The pathway there is humble obedience.

SEPTEMBER 7

Decision-making Under Stress
1 Samuel 13:1-15

Unquestionably, Saul was under real pressure when the powerful Philistines were assembling to fight Israel. Saul's troops were so intimidated that they fled to the caves. Saul feared that if he did not act quickly the whole army would desert. All the while he anxiously waited for Samuel to offer the sacrifices that precede battle to demonstrate Israel's dependence on the Lord.

It was a test case. But at the first moment of strain, Saul was disobedient. We see his desire for independence and his failure to have faith in God. If he had turned to the Lord he would have found relief for his anxiety, but instead he allowed people and circumstances to control him.

Facing stress in life is unavoidable. So is being tested. And God rarely moves as quickly as we wish. Never forget that testing is for our good to strengthen our character and faith. It is allowed by God, who knows what he is doing and why. 'Our urgency and impatience stem from the shortness of our vision and the imperfection of our knowledge of all the facts. God's seeming leisureliness arises from his perfect knowledge of all the facts and his perfect control of all the circumstances' (Author unknown).

SEPTEMBER 8

Faith In The Crisis
1 Samuel 13:16-14:23

We learn from Saul's failure the most important lesson of life: the absolute necessity for obedience to God. In Jonathan, however, we see the room for human endeavour. Indeed, our wholehearted willing service is desirable. The key is to be sure our plans are aligned with the plan of God. Then we are to be strong, go ahead, and do it with all our might.

What gave Jonathan courage was his belief that the significant factor in victory was the power of God, not the size of the army. 'For nothing can hinder the LORD from saving, whether by many or by few' (14:6). His devotion and recognition of God's power contrasted sharply with his father's indecision.

But our faith always needs to be tempered with humility. 'Perhaps the Lord will act on our behalf' does not reveal a lack of faith in God, but a vital humility that acknowledges the human capacity for error. What is God's response to such faith? In answer to the cry of one person, he will harness all of nature to enter the scene of his servant's plight! The Lord God is in control of nature, our enemies, and our limited resources. He delights to do his part - let us be faithful to do ours.

SEPTEMBER 9

Failure Under Pressure
1 Samuel 15:1-35

Once again, Saul compromised in a high-pressured situation by not following the precise instructions God had given for a military campaign. Samuel caught him in the act. At first Saul lied, then made excuses. But Samuel accused Saul of rebelling against God: 'Because you have rejected the word of the LORD, he has rejected you as king' (23). Even after Samuel put Saul's disobedience on the level of idolatry and witchcraft, Saul's show of repentance is more of a desperate appeal to Samuel to help him save face with the crowd. What an extraordinary revelation as to what motivated the man: public opinion mattered more than God's opinion!

There is something desperately sad when a life goes tragically wrong. Saul began with every opportunity and failed to become the man he could have been. Why? Because he lacked a strong compulsion to obey God no matter what. That left him vulnerable to being a people-pleaser rather than a God-pleaser. What folly to seek favour with people, who are fundamentally fickle by nature and who have no real power. Let us do as Paul encourages, 'Fearing God, we persuade men'.

SEPTEMBER 10

Trusting In The Unseen Real
1 Samuel 17

There is no doubt that Goliath was terribly intimidating, but Saul had to make a choice: would he trust in appearances or in the unseen reality of God? His decision to trust in appearances rather than the power of God caused him to become so immobilised that it demoralised his army.

How did David see reality? David clearly knew the danger he was up against, but he believed that beyond appearances was the deeper reality of God. Because he saw the problem through the eyes of faith, he discerned the true nature of the battle. Because Goliath cursed David by his gods, that confirmed to David that this was not a fight between man and man, but between the true God and false gods. David knew that there is no contest between human bravado and the power of God.

Times of testing raise metaphysical questions: Is God there? Is he loving? Is he all-powerful? Because David's answer was categorically 'Yes' he had confidence in God when he needed it most. What enables us to overcome adversity is not sentimental feelings about some vaguely-conceived god, but vital faith in the true God.

SEPTEMBER 11

Do Not Empower The Lie
1 Samuel 17:1-11

Goliath shows us the style and the deception of evil. His arrogance and false self-confidence is the pride that goes before a fall. There is an illusory nature to evil. It attempts to win through bluff - puffing itself up to a horrendous size through intimidation. Its style is frightening, but Saul shows us that if we believe the lie (that human resources determine who wins the battle) we will empower evil. Evil can only be conquered when we believe the truth and trust in God, whose power is greater than evil.

When we are in the midst of battle and feel our courage and faith melting, let us not complain that our resources to fight are inadequate. That is precisely the point! God could have struck down Goliath with a coronary. But God delights in demonstrating his power through our limited resources. What God asks of us is to have faith and courage in him. When we find ourselves embattled let us ask: Is there a lie I am embracing that is empowering evil because of my failure of faith? Victory comes from having courageous faith in the One who longs to fight the battle for us: 'For this is not your battle for the battle is the Lord's'.

The Right Weapons For The Real Battle
1 Samuel 17:38-51

David had more than a sling when he entered his battle with Goliath. The first stone to be slung was not the rock but David's words of *truth*. One word of truth, spoken in the power of the Holy Spirit, flies like a rock to puncture evil's swelled balloon of lies.

His breastplate, while not visible, was defending the *righteousness* of God. His courage came because he was defending God's honour, not his own. His mission was to show that God will protect his children and give them *peace* - even from terrifying enemies. David had no physical shield, but he stepped out in a shield of *faith* when no one else dared. He knew his help had to come from God alone. He did not wear a helmet of metal but of *salvation*, for he believed the purpose of the battle was: 'That *all* this assembly may know there is a true God in Israel'. David is the precursor to Ephesians 6.

Since we 'wrestle not against flesh and blood', it means that spiritually life is war. David shows us that victory comes when we wear weapons that were designed for the nature of the battle. 'You come to me with a sword and a spear, *but I come to you...*'

SEPTEMBER 13

Amazing Grace
1 Samuel 18:1-9

David, unarmed and looking totally vulnerable, had just fought and beaten the heavily-armed Goliath. Then Jonathan made an extravagant gesture. He stripped himself of all his royal insignia and dressed David with his royal armour and weapons. Immediately following, there was a party to celebrate the victory with joyous dancing and singing. But the 'Elder One', Saul, could not celebrate because he was 'very angry'. His jealousy of David made it impossible.

This follows the exact sequence of the parable of the Prodigal Son - a young man comes home stripped and vulnerable but receives the extravagant gesture of being dressed like royalty. The party begins, but the elder brother refuses to participate because he is very angry.

Here are two famous stories in the Bible: one man unclothed and vulnerable due to his great faith, the other stripped and vulnerable due to his great sin. And God dresses them both like royalty! All that God requires for the worst sinner to be dressed like the greatest hero is repentance. Then all are invited to come to the party and to be clothed in his royal robes of righteousness. 'Love so amazing, so divine, demands my life, my soul, my all.'

SEPTEMBER 14

We Demand The Right To Be Wrong

1 Samuel 18:8-19:24

It is significant that Saul began always to keep a spear by his side. The point cannot be missed: people who succumb to deep hatred and jealousy usually feel they are being victimised and that their hatred is justified. Most abusers feel abused. They must fix the blame on someone else and thus they become addicted to their target. What drove Saul was his relentless quest to prove to the world David's guilt, and to aggrandise himself. Hate made him feel self-righteous; it is always hungry for a scapegoat. If he could label someone else as 'bad', then the better he could feel about himself. So long as Saul could pursue and defame David, it relieved his own tension, kept him from looking inward, and momentarily gave him the sense that he was in control.

But deep down Saul knew why everything was going wrong. He had alienated God out of his rebellion and disobedience. But instead of repenting, Saul was determined to prove he was right. Everything was a frantic effort to justify himself, and to foil God's plan. Tragically, he followed evil's inevitable path: the devil may know he has lost - but he still insists he is right!

SEPTEMBER 15

David On The Run
1 Samuel 19:8-12

David had a stupendous victory and was enjoying its fruits. He had the honour and respect of the people, he lived at court, women sang his praises, the king's son was his devoted friend, and Michal loved him. Yet in one chapter he went from being the golden boy to an outlaw. All his favour was replaced by violent slander, he was forced to live like a fugitive off the land, and many previous admirers turned against him out of fear and confusion. In his early flush of glory, he could not have fathomed it.

What are we to learn from this? Life is so transitory. Circumstances can change overnight. To put our trust in professional status, fame or popularity, is a very shaky foundation indeed. Human approval is too unreliable. Rather we must build our lives on the rock of God, who is the *only* one worthy of pleasing, and the only one who will not let us down. We need a godly detachment to live life well. An attitude that recognises, whether in times of blessing or suffering, that there is only one stable, reliable place of safety: trusting in the living God.

God Supplies Our Need
1 Samuel 20

Times of testing not only reveal what is in the heart of one being tested, but they reveal what is in the hearts of others too. Times of crisis bring both profound disappointments in people we thought we could trust and encouraging surprises. We do not need a large army of support during difficult times. But we do need a few servants of God who tell us the truth, give a healing word when our faith falters, and help us recognise the hand of God when we are too embattled to see. While it is vitally important not to be controlled by human approval, the value of Christian friends who care for our comfort *and* our character cannot be overemphasised.

When Jonathan first became bonded to David, David did not have a care in the world. Only God knew how soon Jonathan's friendship would not be a luxury in an already charmed life, but a lifeline to a man in crisis. God knows the trials we will be required to endure. We can count on him to give us the resources we need. David had no idea how much he would need Jonathan's friendship - but he didn't have to. God did, and had already moved on his behalf.

SEPTEMBER 17

The Kingdom Of God
Or The Kingdom Of Self

1 Samuel 18:1-12

What does the Kingdom of God look like? Jonathan showed us as he stripped off his regalia and offered it to David in delightful abandon. The natural thing would be to look to his future, to protect his own turf. Any adviser would say, 'Jonathan, that was *not* a smart career move. We need to assess the damage you've done and devise ways to promote you.' But it was an act of utter unselfishness; joyful, hilarious giving. There wasn't an ounce of self-protection or self-interest. Why? Because his trust was in God - who does a much better job of looking after the interests of self than Jonathan ever could.

What is the Kingdom of Self like? Saul showed us in his inability to celebrate. He could not look outward and rejoice, for he was hopelessly turned in on himself. People could not be valued for their giftedness, but were seen as threats to be competed against.

The picture of the two men says it best: Jonathan standing before David, eyes radiant and beaming, having just given everything away; and Saul having everything, yet looking anxious and furtively holding his spear against any imagined threat. That is the choice: self's kingdom of bondage or God's kingdom of freedom.

SEPTEMBER 18

There Is No Bottom To Evil
1 Samuel 22-23

Saul was clearly deteriorating. He was increasingly self-absorbed, self-deceived and self-pitying. We might dismiss him as merely pathetic, but the story of the massacre of the priests at Nob shows how desperately serious rebellion is. We must never underestimate evil.

Some say it was when they finally hit 'rock-bottom' that their lives turned around. The truth is, there is no bottom to evil. Evil has infinite ways to reinvent itself. God gives an allotted time for the sinner to respond to his grace and repent, or in his mercy he brings justice and judgment. The judgment is not only merciful for those potentially destroyed by the sinner, but it is ultimately merciful to the sinner himself because evil has no limits.

In its nature, rebellion is also deceived. Therefore reason cannot prevail. How often we try to reason with a person in rebellion, to no avail! That is because rebellion is spiritual in nature and irrational. It was the height of irrationality for Saul to kill the priests. He had now effectively cut himself off from God's guidance. What he did was not in his best interests. But sin never is.

SEPTEMBER 19

Wait For God's Timing
1 Samuel 23

If we read between the lines we see a great drama unfolding. We have a story of two leaders locked in a death struggle - with one refusing to fight! We have a king with power, wealth and a professional army of 3,000, fighting a shepherd-warrior, with no wealth, living in the wilderness with a band of 600 outlaws and family members. David's greatest challenge was how *not* to fight Saul. Twice Saul fell into David's hands. David refused to kill him, believing it would violate God's will. God had promised David he would be king. David's challenge was to wait for God's timing and to trust him, no matter how bad the situation.

Humanly, David's position was desperate. Survival was not easy. Yet look at how God protected him! Saul pursued David to the same area, the same mountain, and even to the same cave. When 3,000 of Saul's men could not find David, Jonathan apparently had no trouble! It requires an act of faith to believe God is overruling our lives. Often we only see it in retrospect. But he is using every difficulty to build our character and our faith. God is there and he is able.

How To Treat An Enemy
1 Samuel 24

David faced Saul for the first time since he escaped. His argument was clear: he was not Saul's enemy. His evidence was convincing since he had just resisted the opportunity to kill Saul. David asked the Lord to judge this case. He would trust God to vindicate and to deliver him from evil. David seemed to imply that Saul had taken on more than he realised - Saul had taken on the Lord, who would show David to be in the right.

David shows us how to treat an enemy. He never spoke ill of Saul though Saul slandered him. He always showed respect for his office, even when Saul's person had nothing to recommend itself. He spoke the truth to Saul when the time was appropriate. But even then he made his points with respect and dignity, without sarcasm or anger. He showed mercy when Saul asked him to. Most importantly, David knew that his vindication would come from God, not himself. The temptation to defend himself must have been great. But rarely does that approach do any good anyway. It would only have brought David down into the cesspool with Saul.

David modelled Jesus: 'When reviled, he reviled not again, but entrusted himself to him who judges justly.'

SEPTEMBER 21

Temptation: New Faces - Old Tricks
1 Samuel 24:1-7

God told David that one day he would be king. Yet there is David constantly foraging for food in the desert! Saul entered the cave and David's men told David to kill him. The reason is obvious: then the power and the kingdom would be his for the taking. They made their appeal through spiritual logic, even quoting the Lord. David refused to disobey God.

Jesus was also tempted when he was in the desert. His identity, too, had been affirmed by God but challenged by the tempter's statement, 'If you are the Son of God...' Likewise, David's identity was challenged by his men's assumption that it would be their verdict, not God's, as to who would become king. Jesus, like David, was encouraged to take the authority and power that was rightfully his, but to take it now. And the enemy quoted the Lord, just as David's men did. David rebuked the men; Jesus sent the devil away.

Somehow it is reassuring to know how little the enemy's tactics have changed. Always look for the hand at work behind the temptation. Saul was only a pawn of David's real enemy. Once you discern the real source of evil, then 'resist the devil, and he will flee from you.'

SEPTEMBER 22

Holiness Is A Habit

1 Samuel 25:1-13

Nabal modelled how to insult someone with skill. He was not only unkind but his comments were designed to offend and humiliate David. What was David's response? 'Put on your swords!' How could David have endured so much from Saul, and let Nabal, who is at best a 'diminutive Saul', get to him? Because his testing with Saul was well-known ground. He had been cultivating wisdom and restraint for a long time.

Once we know the area where we are being tested and what the terrain is like - the temptations and counter-strategies necessary to resist - it is far easier to practise godliness. But Nabal caught David off-guard, and thus we get a glimpse of what David is capable of without godly restraint.

It takes practice to develop godly habits. The 'habit' God is developing in David is not treating his enemies as they treat him. He is learning the importance of not avenging himself, but entrusting his cause to God. The Lord will bring justice and judgment, for he is a God who rewards good and judges evil. Let us not be discouraged when we fail, having thought we had conquered that area already. Godliness is not acquired in a weekend - it takes practice and perseverance.

SEPTEMBER 23

Live By Faith, Not Impulses
1 Samuel 25:14-31

If Nabal shows us how to insult someone with skill, then Abigail models how to deal with an enraged person *par excellence*. She responded to the situation with total humility. Physically, she bowed prostrate before David in obeisance. Verbally, she referred to David as 'my lord', and herself as 'your handmaid'. Her behaviour caused an entire army to stop in its tracks!

In a highly volatile situation with complex dynamics, Abigail succeeded in lowering the emotional temperature and averting a disastrous plan of action. How? Her genius and spiritual power was in demonstrating the opposite spiritual counterpart to the sin expressed. In the presence of pride she showed deep humility; in contrast to David's desire for revenge due to the injustice, Abigail asked that the injustice fall upon her. Let God settle the score!

Abigail shows us that 'turning the other cheek' is not accomplished by being weak, but by taking spiritual authority. First, by properly identifying the sin, then by demonstrating the counterpart fruit of the Spirit. There can be powerful results when we respond to the Spirit and not our impulses!

SEPTEMBER 24

On Having Divine Objectivity
1 Samuel 25:23-31

How do we get discernment when we have been criticised? Abigail shows us it is through having divine objectivity. First, we must consider the source of the criticism. Is the person criticising someone whose opinion matters to us? It is foolish not to listen to the correction of someone we respect. But Abigail's argument to David was that he must not be offended by a man with a character like Nabal's!

Second, our reputation is in God's hands. Let him bring judgment and promotion according to his timetable, not ours. Abigail recognised that David would make a contribution to the Kingdom for a long time. When God chose to reinstate David, after his time of testing, she did not want him to have a marred record from having responded foolishly.

Third, consider the style of the criticism. Remember that God convicts and Satan condemns. God never corrects us in ways that produce despair or self-loathing - but hope and peace. And God will correct us in a way that we can 'hear'. Looking at the styles of Nabal and Abigail, it is not difficult to discern what power was operating behind them. Never listen to the Enemy's accusations. Always listen to God's correction.

SEPTEMBER 25

Not Perfection But A Teachable Spirit
1 Samuel 25:13,32-35

David rallied four hundred men to join him in attacking Nabal. Outraged, he proclaimed that God should punish him if he failed to destroy Nabal. He was convinced that he was right and that God agreed with him. Imagine telling a man in this frame of mind that he is dead wrong! Yet that is exactly what Abigail did, albeit with extraordinary skill and tact, and in full view of his men.

Remember, David had a lot riding on not wanting to appear foolish. Yet he responded by praising God for her good judgment in clear contrast to his own! There was no attempt to save face.

God does not require perfection; we could not produce it anyway. What he requires is a teachable spirit that is quick to own mistakes and learn from them. The critical issue is how we respond to our problem once we see it. David responded with delight and gratitude for having been corrected because it kept him from exacerbating the problem. Perhaps the 'unforgivable sin' is the sin of insisting that we are not sinners! God cannot forgive the sin that we refuse to admit.

SEPTEMBER 26

Forgiveness Versus Reconciliation
1 Samuel 26

Again David had the opportunity to kill Saul. Having seen God's clear judgment upon Nabal, David was even more resolute that he had to wait for providence to decide Saul's fate. However, Saul expressed remorse and begged David to be reconciled. David chose not to. Why?

Because David had seen enough to know that Saul's words of remorse were merely part of the cycle. Saul was always sorry when he got caught. But in time his abusive behaviour would emerge worse than ever. When David compared Saul's actions and words, his verdict was, 'His words were smooth as butter, but there was murder in his heart'. If Saul's repentance was genuine, he would have done it privately, not publicly. There would need to be sustained behavioural change for David to know it was authentic, and he was safe.

David understood a crucial distinction. He forgave Saul, just as we must forgive our enemies. But he did not confuse forgiveness with reconciliation. He could not reconcile because there had been no repentance. For David to have reconciled with unrepentant Saul would have meant he was reconciling to evil! Reconciliation on any other basis than repentance is fraudulent. Christian unity only has meaning, and honours God, when it is done in truth.

SEPTEMBER 27

The Failure To Appropriate Grace

1 Samuel 28, 31

Saul's downfall was not inevitable. It came from repeated rejections of instructions from God, and his stubborn refusal to admit wrong and repent. Saul exemplifies the tragedy and paradox of rebellion. The more he deified human will over against submitting to God's will, the weaker he became. His wilfulness left him a jellyfish of a man.

Yet, men risked their lives to capture his corpse because they recognised his worth. Samuel, David, and even the Lord, grieved over Saul. They grieved because they knew he could have been a great man had he submitted to God. They grieved not for the man he was, but for the man he might have been.

That means there are no cardboard enemies in life. An enemy has a greater identity than the person who did that bad thing to us. An enemy is a person created in God's image, with dignity and potential greatness. David always recognised that Saul was behaving as less than he was created to be.

We cannot accurately evaluate lives in rebellion against God by merely looking at their sins. It is their failure to have appropriated grace - the good they could have done, the people they might have been. That is the even greater tragedy.

SEPTEMBER 28

Faith In Adversity
1 Samuel 29, 30

The measure of a person is seen in how he handles adversity. There are many temptations in adversity: subtly blaming God for the problem, justifying or defending oneself to others, etc. David fell into none of these traps. Instead, 'David strengthened himself in the LORD his God'.

David reminds us that being a believer, or a future king, does not protect us from the ambiguities of life. 'The rain falls on the just and the unjust.' Knowing God does not protect us from the storm, but we *are* protected from the storm's power to destroy us. Indeed, God will use the very suffering to forge our character and strengthen our faith. He will enable us to trust his sovereignty at a deeper level.

But we must do our part. We need to be realistic about the fact that life is difficult. Instead of blaming God for our trials, we must turn to him, who alone can give us the resources we need to overcome. Let's follow David's example as we walk through life's difficulties: pouring out our honest feelings about our situation, but to the One who loves us, who is there for us, and who longs to demonstrate that he will never let his children down. Not ever.

SEPTEMBER 29

Lessons In The Wilderness
Summary of 1 Samuel

The Lord led David into the wilderness, just as he led the Israelites and would lead Jesus. Why did the Lord put David through the paces like this? Because God looks on the heart. He knows that nothing reveals what is in the heart, and roots out what should not be there, like times of testing.

David learned invaluable lessons during the wilderness years. He learned humbly to admit his faults. He knew that God was king. David learned that following God was no passport to an easy life. But he could find all the resources he needed for life's difficulties in God. He discovered that obstacles were God's opportunity to answer the prayers of his servant!

What if God had spared David all the trauma of the wilderness years? Then David would have never achieved the same insight, wisdom and character. No doubt most of the psalms would not have been written! David shows us that God will use every difficulty, every tear shed to his glory. Yes, David's suffering was very real. But his suffering was not the last word. God always has the last word - a word of life, healing and hope to the broken, the wounded and the suffering.

SEPTEMBER 30

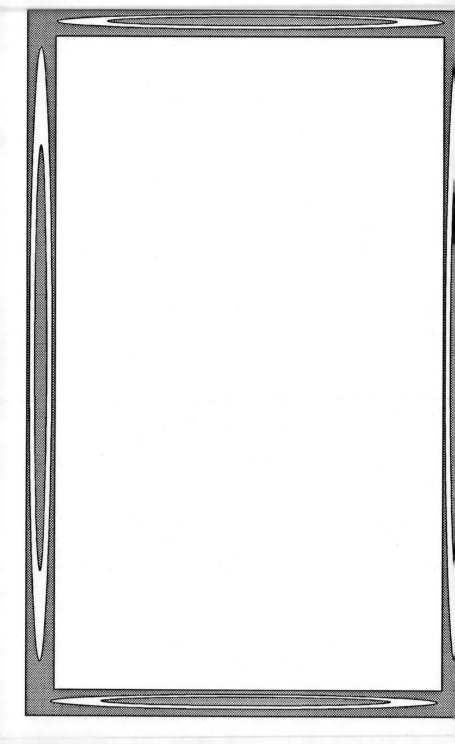

OCTOBER

JOHN CAIGER

*The God
Who Provides*

Look At The Birds...
Matthew 6:25-34

Jesus is telling his disciples that one of their happy privileges is freedom from worry. There is no need to worry. We can see from the way God provides for the birds and the flowers that he is perfectly able to provide for us.

God feeds the birds and clothes the flowers - very beautiful, but quite humble, members of his creation. So is it possible that he will fail to look after his children? Men, through their fall into evil, make things difficult for the birds, for flowers and for themselves. But God has so arranged the world we live in that there are resources enough to feed and clothe all his creatures, if only they will learn to use his gifts as he intends them to.

So Jesus said, 'Look at the birds of the air... See how the lilies of the field grow.' They live within the pattern ordained for them by the Creator, and as they do this the birds find their food and the flowers grow beautiful. It is as we discover the way of trustful dependence on God that our needs will be supplied and our lives clothed with beauty too.

OCTOBER 1

The Nesting Of The Sparrow
Psalm 84:1-4

Jesus told us to look at the birds, not only to study their make-up and their ways, but chiefly to discover all we can about the Creator who designed them.

We soon discover that birds need homes and nests as well as food, and God has given them the most marvellous ingenuity in finding a home and in building a nest. This beautiful psalm tells us of the sparrow and the swallow doing this in the forecourt of God's temple, each of them discovering the place for their home near the great altar of sacrifice.

No one drove them away or robbed or disturbed their nests. The eggs were not stolen. The baby birds were not molested. Each little family was perfectly safe 'near God's altar'. And the psalmist argues from this, just as Jesus did in his sermon, that if there is a place of safety and peace in God's house for the sparrow and the swallow, how much more can his children expect to find security and spiritual satisfaction when they make their home in his presence! To dwell 'in the secret place of the Most High' is to 'abide under the shadow of the Almighty' (Psalm 91:1).

OCTOBER 2

Look At This Lonely Sparrow!
Psalm 102:1-8

This poor man was in great trouble - physical discomfort, loss of appetite, loneliness, and enemies who maligned him. His world was falling to pieces. He felt 'like an owl among the ruins'. Sleepless on his bed he seemed like a lonely bird on a housetop - and the word he used was the word for 'sparrow' in Psalm 84:3.

'Consider the birds,' Jesus said. So why was that sparrow perched on that housetop alone? It had its enemies too. Maybe a cat had been stalking it in the garden below. It was shaken and frightened - and there was nothing to eat on the housetop! What could it do? After it had collected its wits, it would spread its little wings and fly. It would find company and food with other sparrows in the field nearby.

The lesson is clear. When we feel like the sparrow, frightened and lonely, we must use our wings of faith and prayer and love for God and men. We must rise above our difficulties, find help in Christian company, and receive fresh supplies of comfort and spiritual energy from God who renews our strength to do just this.

OCTOBER 3

'Two A Penny - Five For Twopence!'
Matthew 10:29-31

According to Jesus this was the market price of sparrows in his day. They were not expensive. In Luke 12:6 he tells us that if you were prepared to spend twopence you would have one free! So it wouldn't cost you much to buy a sparrow!

Yet what does Jesus say about the value of the sparrows? Not one of them is forgotten by God! 'Not one of them will fall to the ground apart from the will of your Father.' There is a place for each sparrow in his providential care. In a fallen world like ours, baby sparrows topple out of nests and fall to their death, but even this has its place in the mystery of God's sovereign control.

And if this is true for them, how much more is it true for us? A recent translation reads, 'There is no need to be afraid; you are worth more than hundreds of sparrows.' Who would want to buy a sparrow? Yet God has bought us - and at what a price! The price he paid to redeem us from evil was the sacrifice and death of his Son. So how much must we be worth to him?

OCTOBER 4

Looking For The New Earth
Genesis 8:6-7

Noah had been cooped up for six months in the ark, when the flood-water began to recede, and the great ship came to rest on the Ararat mountains. Soon the mountain tops were visible; and after six weeks, Noah sent out a scout to survey the scene. He chose a raven, a powerful bird, able to go without food for long periods of time. But the scout did not report back!

It kept flying back and forth until the water had drained and the earth had dried. What patience it had! What disciplined endurance - to keep flying without food in the determined expectation that out of that vast watery ruin the earth would reappear. We mustn't credit the raven with too much theological insight - but it never gave up its flying until the new home it looked for had appeared.

What an example and an incentive that raven is for us! For God has promised us a new heaven and a new earth, and we must use our wings of faith and prayer and love to keep up above the perilous waters of our ruined world in expectation of the appearing of our new home.

OCTOBER 5

A Divine Commission
1 Kings 17:2-6

Like all God's creatures the raven is subject to the will of its Creator. The various birds and beasts which were to enter the ark 'came' to Noah. Three times we are told this. Noah did not have to hunt them down and catch them - they came to him. And they came because God brought them. In the same way the Lord ordered ravens to feed Elijah and gave them their timetable for his morning and evening meals.

This is a sensational example of the ability of our Father in heaven to provide for his children in their times of special need. It was a miracle, and miracles don't usually happen. But God can move miraculously whenever he pleases. There is nothing he cannot do.

What privileged ravens they were! They were particularly chosen for this most special service to be a bearer of God's help, and it is a high privilege for us when God chooses us to minister in any way to the needs of his servants. The highest privilege of all, I suppose, is when the Lord says to a man he is sending to teach his hungry people, 'I have ordered you to feed them there.'

OCTOBER 6

'Consider The Ravens...'
Luke 12:22-26

Jesus was speaking about anxiety. He often did. He said it is one of the thorny shrubs which spring up and choke God's Word in our hearts. He counselled emphatically against it - here especially with the simple command, 'Do not worry'.

By way of illustration, Jesus pointed to the ravens. It is not in their power to sow seed or reap, and they have 'no storeroom or barn'. Yet God feeds them. The argument is: if God can provide ravens with food, he can also feed us. Other scriptures bear witness to this too. 'He provides food for the cattle and for the young ravens when they call' (Psalm 147:9). 'Who provides food for the raven when its young cry out to God...?' (Job 38:41).

This does not mean that we do nothing, and God puts food into our mouths! The ravens find food by searching for it. They do what God created them to do. So must we. We must work for our food. That is how God made us. And as we play our part, using our gifts and doing our duty, we shall find what we need.

Do not worry!

OCTOBER 7

On Eagles' Wings...
Deuteronomy 32:9-12

Moses pictures the Lord in the image of the eagle - the mother eagle! The brood of eaglets are snug in the nest. The mother bird hovers over them, drops suddenly, seizes one, lifts it from the nest, flies with it in her beak beyond the lip of the crag and drops it into thin air. It plummets helplessly down. The eagle swoops under it, catches it on her great pinions, rises above the crag - and repeats the process again and again, until the baby bird, making instinctive use of its little wings, finds itself afloat in the air and learning to fly.

The experience seems devastating for the eaglet, but it is the way the young bird is trained to soar on the air currents, and to be conformed to the majestic image of the monarch of the skies. Moses sees the whole procedure as a dramatic picture of God's ways in the care and training of his people to do his will - and to become like him! The Lord uses the imagery himself in Exodus 19:4, 'I carried you on eagles' wings and brought you to myself.' So this is a most prestigious illustration.

Wings
Isaiah 40:27-31

It is a characteristic of birds that (with rare exceptions) they are able to fly. They can rise above the earthly level of things - above the beasts and the reptiles and the insects, even above earth-bound humanity. When men fly they do it by the use of immensely sophisticated machines, but birds do it by the use of powers within themselves. They have wings.

Christians, too, are able to rise. In the spiritual dimension where there are dark depths of fearful peril into which people easily slip and fall, Christians have wings on which they are able to mount up into clear skies and sunlit heavens. Faith and hope and love are all wings which, in the energies of the Holy Spirit, can be used to lift us into communion with Christ and with God.

And the image which Isaiah employs is not that of the little birds that flutter, not even of the bigger birds that swoop and glide, but of the eagle whose great pinions lift it so high it can scarcely be tracked by unaided human eyes. Those who hope in the Lord find their strength renewed so that their spirits can soar into heavenly places.

OCTOBER 9

Who hath blessed us with all spiritual blessings in heavenly places in Christ. Ephesians 1: 3.

A Joy that can never be diminished. John 15: 11.
A Glory that can never be clouded. Romans 8: 18.
A Light that cannot be darkened. John 8: 12.
A Rest that cannot be disturbed. Matthew 11: 28, 29.
Resources that cannot be over-drawn. Ephesians 3: 20.

...ng Of Youth

...03:1-5

...f the Old Testament has a ...passage. It reads: 'like an ...nd vigour after moulting'. ...en the great birds begin to ...rag, way above menace or ...shed their feathers. In the ...d lose their power to fly. It ...eble and dependent condi- ...red for by its latest brood ...e time new feathers begin ...ength returns. The body of ... wings are filled with new power. When the process is complete the eagle rises with full vigour in the beat of its pinions and is able to soar into high heaven again.

What a picture this is of the goodness and kindness of the Lord who satisfies our desires with good things so that our youth is renewed like the eagle's! It is our youthfulness of spirit that is in view, and God who is spirit is himself the source of this renewal of our powers.

What The Dove Is Seeking
Genesis 8:8-12

The dove is the New Testament symbol of the Holy Spirit - the divine comforter and guide, sent by the Father and the Son to bring heavenly grace into the lives of people like ourselves.

Noah sent the dove out of the ark to find a home for itself where it could rest, but the first time the water of judgment covered everything. A second time it flew and came back with an olive leaf in its beak. It was the message of judgment past and new life springing. The third time the dove did not return - it had at last found a place where it could rest.

The dove is a homing bird. It flies to the place where it is at home, and the home it is seeking is the heart to which Jesus has spoken his peace and to which he has given his rest. 'If anyone loves me,' said Jesus, 'he will obey my teaching. My Father will love him, and we will come to him and make our home with him.' And Jesus was speaking of the Holy Spirit through whom the presence of the Father and the Son is made known.

OCTOBER 11

The Dove In The Life Of Jesus
Luke 3:21-22

It is most comforting and reassuring to notice the gentle quality of each of the designations given in the Bible to the persons of the Holy Trinity. The first is the Father, the source of all being; the second is the Lamb, given in sacrifice for the saving of the world; and the third is the Dove. No wonder the Scriptures speak of the Lord's 'loving-kindness and tender mercies', of the gentleness of Jesus and of a fruit of the Spirit being gentleness!

And Jesus, the Son of God made man, was evidently filled with the Holy Spirit from the moment he was born. He was then anointed with a special visitation of the power of the Spirit, symbolised by the descent of the dove, and every part of his ministry in the world was declared to be under the authority of the Spirit - his birth, his baptism, his temptation, his teaching, his miracles, his death, and his ministry to his apostles in the days immediately following his resurrection.

The Dove was perfectly at home in the life and ministry of the Lamb, and the Lamb was strengthened, directed and inspired by the presence in him of the Dove.

OCTOBER 12

The Dove In The Christian
Song of Songs 2:14

This fascinating love-song has been interpreted by Jews and Christians alike to speak to us of the relationship between our heavenly husband and ourselves as his people and his bride.

In this verse the bridegroom is calling his bride, as a dove, to come out of hiding and to show herself to him. He wants to see her face and to hear her voice, for to him her voice is sweet and her face is lovely.

It is the character of the dove that Jesus looks for in us. He tells us to be as innocent and harmless as doves; and the dove in the Bible is the symbol of the Spirit of gentleness, of peace, and of sacrifice. When Joseph and Mary offered their sacrifice to God for Jesus, they offered a pair of doves. So Jesus by the Holy Spirit offered himself in sacrifice to God.

Our heavenly bridegroom looks for the fruit of his Spirit in us. He gives us the Spirit to reproduce in us the freshness and beauty of his own life and character, and he rejoices to see in our faces, and to hear in our voices, a constantly increasing likeness to himself.

The Most High - The Mother Hen!
Psalm 91:1-4

The image of the mother bird is introduced again - this time that of the humble hen sheltering her young under her wings.

Jesus, in his lament over Jerusalem, used heart-rending words: '...how often I have longed to gather your children together, as a hen gathers her chicks under her wings, but you were not willing.' Not willing to confide in the one to whom we most closely belong, or to find shelter in the person who understands and can safeguard us best!

The psalmist's testimony is that all who dwell in the shelter of the Most High will be covered with his feathers, so that under his wings they may find refuge.

There is a story of a farmyard which was swept with fire. In a corner a hen was found sitting, her feathers charred and her life lost in the overwhelming heat. But when the farmer touched her with his foot, her chicks ran out from under her burned wings, unharmed and full of life. There is a parable here of the refuge we find in the Saviour who died to save us! This hen-like image of God is full of gospel grace and truth.

OCTOBER 14

The Flight Of The Birds
Jeremiah 4:23-26 with 9:10

We live on the edge of London where birds are plenti-
ful - near Kew Gardens and Richmond's Great Park.
But one winter day, all was curiously still. The weather
was bitter, the ground hard with frost, the air damp and
penetrating, and nature generally inhospitable. And
there was not a bird to be seen of any kind. It was a
desolate feeling!

Jeremiah associates the flight of the birds with the
pouring out of God's judgment on our wicked earth -
and I thought of the Day that is to come when God will
judge the world and destroy its evil. We are told in
Matthew 24:30,31 that, as a dramatic preliminary to
that Day, the Lord Jesus will appear in power and glory
with his angels, who will be sent with a loud trumpet
call to 'gather his elect from the four winds, from one
end of the heavens to the other'. This will be the flight
of the saints from the destruction of the world - to join
the Saviour in his glory and to made fully like him. It
will be the final desolation of our fallen earth when the
saints have all flown into heaven.

OCTOBER 15

'Fix Your Thoughts On Jesus...'
Hebrews 2:14-3:1

From considering the birds (in obedience to the words of Jesus), we turn now to consider Jesus himself. Who and what was he?

We must correct our question first of all. It is not 'who and what was he?', but 'who and what is he?' This letter to the Hebrews was written a generation after Jesus lived and died, so we are at once confronted with matters of supernatural power and mystery.

Jesus is not dead now, but living in 'the power of an indestructible life'. He is in heaven in the place of supreme majesty and authority - at the right hand of God's eternal throne. But he is not remote from us. He is ruling all things in the interests of his church and he is still 'the apostle and high priest whom we confess'.

As our apostle he teaches us all we need to know about God and his kingdom - and all that he teaches us is true. As our high priest he pleads the power of his sacrifice before the heavenly throne to secure our pardon, our acceptance, and our destiny of glory with his Father. So Jesus is the one on whom we fix our thoughts.

OCTOBER 16

'Let Us Fix Our Eyes On Jesus...'
Hebrews 12:1-3

The Christian life is pictured here as a race. The course has been marked out for us so we have no excuse for running off the track. And we are told to strip ourselves of every unnecessary weight and to avoid the self-indulgence which will rob us of our peak condition for running.

It is a long race, and so the runner cannot have the tape in sight all the time, but he will have it in mind always. His heart is set on it, and to reach it he gives every ounce of energy and effort. Both the goal and the prize of the Christian race is Jesus. We cannot see him now with our bodily eyes, but 'the eyes of our heart' (Ephesians 1:18) must be fixed continually on him.

We must hold in our hearts the thought of what he suffered to save us, and of the glory into which the Father has received him at his right hand. Nothing will stimulate and strengthen us so much to face the spite and antagonism of a sinful world as this inward visitation of Jesus, our suffering sin-bearer and our glorious sovereign and friend.

OCTOBER 17

'Here Is My Servant'
Isaiah 42:1-4

We are considering Jesus, the carpenter of Nazareth, the Saviour of the world. Listen to what God says about him. Surprisingly simple, gentle, powerful things!

He is God's chosen one and the focus of his delight. He is the one on whom God's Spirit rests (which is what Messiah means), and who in the Spirit's power will bring justice to the nations. Yet he is a person of such quality that, though invested with illimitable power, he does not shout or bluster or make a noise or a fuss, but deals gently and sensitively with the bruised reed and encourages the smouldering wick to burn more brightly.

He is the Lord's servant - born in a stable, cradled in a feeding trough, reared in a village carpenter's home, speaking to multitudes in a way no other man ever did, performing stupendous works of power as though they came naturally to him (which, of course, they did), taking a towel and a basin to wash the feet of his friends, accepting the death of a criminal in the most extreme humiliation and agony: and all this to lift sinners from squalor to glory.

No wonder God said, 'Here is my servant, whom I uphold.'

OCTOBER 18

'Here Is The Man!'
John 19:1-7

When the Son of God came down from heaven to save the world he was made man! He did not merely clothe his deity in a human body. 'He shared in our humanity' (Hebrews 2:14) - body, soul and spirit. 'He had to be made like his brothers in every way,' and he 'has been tempted in every way, just as we are - yet without sin' (Hebrews 2:17 and 4:15).

So, having been miraculously conceived by the Spirit in the womb of the virgin, he was born in due time as all babies are born, nursed and fed and washed and changed, nurtured and cared for through all the phases of babyhood, boyhood, adolescence and early manhood, in Bethlehem, Egypt and Nazareth. And as a man he needed food and sleep, he rejoiced and he wept, he loved and he suffered, he was buffeted and spat on, flogged and mocked, crowned with thorns, nailed to a cross, and, more quickly than his executioners expected, died, and his body was buried.

All this he suffered, never ceasing to be God the Son, offering his spotless manhood to the death we deserved, thereby opening to us his heavenly kingdom.

OCTOBER 19

'Here Is Your King!'

John 19:12-16

For hundreds of years the Jews had expected a king - to sit on the throne of David, to reign over the house of Jacob, to fulfil God's promises to Abraham and therefore to rule the world.

The promises were there, and the Jews were right to expect him, but they had developed through the centuries a seriously defective idea of the kind of king he would be, and the kind of kingdom over which he is to rule. They thought of him in terms of worldly patterns of kingship. So when he came they didn't recognise him.

Jesus said to Pilate, 'My kingdom is not of this world. If it were, my servants would fight to prevent my arrest by the Jews. But now my kingdom is from another place.' The kingdom he inaugurated, and of which he so often spoke, is the kingdom of heaven. It is the kingdom of God, which means the area in creation in which God manifests his presence and rules in the hearts of his people. It is the kingdom 'of righteousness, peace and joy in the Holy Spirit', and it is characterised by Jesus riding into Jerusalem on the foal of a donkey.

OCTOBER 20

'Here Is Your God!'
Isaiah 40:9-11

Isaiah was speaking about John the Baptist. He heard a voice crying to God's people to prepare the way for him. The glory of the Lord would appear so that all mankind would see it. And the prophet, inspired by the prospect of the coming of the Lord, cried, 'Lift up your voice with a shout... say to the towns of Judah, "Here is your God!" '

It actually happened in the little town of Bethlehem when the glory of the Lord shone around the shepherds and an angel declared that the divine Saviour had been born. The angel Gabriel had told Mary that her child would be called the Son of God. And the Son (as we should expect) shares the nature and life and power and glory of his Father, so that when Jesus attained his full stature as a man, he was able to say, to the fury of his critics, 'I and the Father are one'. When the apostle John described his coming, he wrote, 'The Word became flesh and lived for a while among us... and the Word was God.'

So we worship and adore him of whom the Spirit says, 'Here is your God!'

OCTOBER 21

'*Look, The Lamb of God!*'

John 1:29-34

When John was given a vision of the throne in heaven, he saw a Lamb, looking as if it had been slain; a Lamb who had conquered death (since he was standing), and who was described by one of the heavenly elders as the Lion who has triumphed.

In the Bible, the lamb is the gentle symbol of sacrifice - sacrifice to take away sin, and to reconcile the sinner to God. And Jesus is that sacrifice. Every other lamb slain in sacrifice spoke of him. The lion, of course, is the king of beasts, the embodiment of majesty and power, and Jesus is the lion-like Lamb who has broken the power of 'that ancient serpent, the great dragon' and crushed his head.

So when John the Baptist cried, 'Look, the Lamb of God!' he was able also to say, 'who takes away the sin of the world.' And he could go further and say, 'This is he who baptises with the Holy Spirit,' and further still to say, 'This is the Son of God.'

Jesus is God's Lamb, our sin-bearer, the giver of God's Spirit, God's Son.

OCTOBER 22

'I Am The Good Shepherd'
John 10:11-16

Jesus is speaking here about himself. It is usually not a good sign when people talk about themselves, but Jesus was entitled to do this. It was essential that he should, because in his person as the God-man, and in his mission as the Saviour, he had to declare himself to the world as the only way of approach and welcome and acceptance in the presence of the Father.

That Jesus is a shepherd is obviously important, because he often spoke of himself in this way. And he highlighted the fact that he is the Good Shepherd by contrasting himself with thieves and robbers who come only to steal and destroy, and with hired hands who do not own the sheep but who work merely for self-interest and payment.

But Jesus knows each of his sheep by name. He owns them and has died to rescue them from the wolf. He lives to save his sheep from wandering, and gives them eternal life to share with himself. He holds every sheep in his hand, and he and his hands are held fast in the hand of his Father. So we could not be safer than we are in him.

Here Is Your Life-Giver!
John 4:10-14

In two famous passages in John's Gospel Jesus speaks of himself as the source of living water. And living water, for the Jews of Jesus' day and for Christians of our own, stands for the Holy Spirit.

In John 4:14 Jesus offers a thirsty woman the water of his Spirit, with the promise that this will become in her 'a spring of water welling up to eternal life'. A spring of pure, sweet water, never drying up, rising into the desert of a parched and barren life - isn't that beautiful?

In John 7:37-39 the imagery is the same but a little more developed. Streams of living water are now not only rising in the heart of the believer, but flowing from him, making him the channel of the renewing and refreshing influences and ministries of the Holy Spirit.

And the simplicity of it is staggering! We need the water. Jesus has it to give. So he calls us to come to him and drink it. We have to learn how to drink; though drinking is so simple, a baby knows how!

May the Holy Spirit teach us the simplicity of a thirst that is quenched in him.

Here Is Your Bridegroom!
Matthew 9:14,15

As with many of the claims Jesus made, his references to his being the bridegroom are an assertion of his deity. In the Old Testament the bridegroom or the husband of the people of God is the Lord, Jehovah, the eternal I AM. So when Jesus claims to be the bridegroom, he is declaring that his relationship to his people is divine.

In introducing his parable in Matthew 22 he gives us an extremely beautiful perspective in which to interpret his Father's good news to the world: 'The kingdom of heaven is like a king who prepared a wedding banquet for his son.' So Jesus is the heavenly bridegroom, the church is his holy bride, and the Father is arranging the wedding!

The picture is marvellously rich. The heart of Jesus is full of the bridegroom's love, patience and joy; a willingness to give himself utterly for and to the beloved, and to do all that is needed to prepare her for her union with him. And the prospect of this union is one of light and happy glory with him in the presence of the Father and of the angels, in a home he has himself gone to prepare.

OCTOBER 25

Here Is The Sower!

Matthew 13:37-39

Why in the world do we need a sower? The establishing of a kingdom is a matter for statesmen, technocrats, administrators and computer programmers, isn't it? It depends what kind of kingdom you have in mind.

When life is the basic element, you cannot have a kingdom at all without seed. How does God reveal his glory in the vegetable and animal kingdoms of our world? It is by the sowing and fructifying of seed. Humanity itself could not exist without the sowing of seed. And this principle is just as essentially true in the kingdom of heaven, the kingdom of the Spirit and of God.

To enter the kingdom, Jesus said, 'You must be born again,' and birth is the fruit of the sowing of seed. The seed, Jesus also said, is the Word of God; either sown in the heart of a sinner, or sown in the world in the life of believers in whom it is bearing fruit.

So we need the heavenly sower to scatter the seed of his Word in our hearts, that it may take root and produce the fruit of his Spirit. This is how Christians grow.

OCTOBER 26

'I Am The Vine'

John 15:1-5

God created Israel to be his vine bearing the fruit of his life in the world for its healing. He looked for a crop of good grapes, but, alas, it yielded only bad fruit. So he sent his Son into the world to be what Israel had failed to be - the true vine - so that in him people of all nations could enjoy the secret of the sweetness of the life of their Creator.

Jesus calls people into union with himself: to be joined to him, to live in him, to grow out of him, and to bear fruit for him as branches of the heavenly vine. His life is in every branch, producing the most modest of blossoms but the richest of fruit. The fruit is the reproduction of his own life, the manifestation of his character and disposition in those who live in him. So he was able to say that for us to bear much fruit is to his Father's glory. Of course - because the Father sees the beauty of the vine in the clusters on every branch. And the fruit is not for the branch to enjoy, but for the Father and for his world.

'I Am The Bread'

John 6:32-35

Jesus had fed a huge crowd by miraculously multiplying five small barley loaves and two small fish. The people were understandably astonished. There was a tradition that when the Messiah came he would feed multitudes just as Moses had done. Could Jesus be the Messiah?

The crowd came again and asked if Jesus would do what Moses had done. Jesus told them it was not Moses, but his Father, who had given them manna from heaven. And he went on to say that he had come from heaven, not just to give them bread for their bodies, but to be to them, in person, the spiritual bread that God was giving to bring new life to the world.

It seemed unbelievable that this carpenter from Nazareth should be saying such things, but Jesus gave them still greater challenges to faith. He claimed to be the arbiter of the resurrection, promising eternal life to those who believe in him. He offered himself as living bread for a man to eat and live for ever. To believe in him is to receive a life which death can never touch.

Here is the gospel in the clearest and most glorious terms.

OCTOBER 28

'The Lamb Is Its Lamp'

Revelation 21:23

John is writing of his vision of the Holy City, which is the bride, the wife of the Lamb. The symbols are piled one upon another to give us powerful impressions of the glory and beauty of the new world which God will create to be his dwelling with his redeemed and dearly-loved children.

Not surprisingly it is full of the light of the glory of God. Glory is the perfection of a thing - its radiance, its fullness, its total freedom from defect or blemish or stain. So heaven will be vibrant with God's power, pregnant with his purposes, and suffused with the Spirit of his goodness, beauty and truth.

His glory shines everywhere - and the Lamb is its lamp. This surely means that it is through the Lamb, our glorified Lord Jesus, that the light of God's glory streams. It is in him that it is concentrated, and it is from him that we receive the pure and perfect illumination by which we enjoy all that heaven holds for us.

Jesus was the light of this world when he was here, and he is the lamp which fills the world to come with a glory undimmed and undying.

OCTOBER 29

'*I Am The Gate*'

John 10:7-9

There are teachings in our world today - often, sadly, in so-called Christian churches - which want us to believe that there are multitudes of gates to lead God's sheep into safety. As all roads in the Roman empire are said to have led to the Imperial City, so teachings and experiences of radically different kinds are said to lead all men ultimately to God.

But the teaching of Jesus about himself in this respect is as clear as the day. He does not present himself as one among a multitude of prophets and teachers, each of whom plays his (or her) part in leading humanity to union with God. On the contrary, he declares himself to be the one and only way by which lost, corrupted, wandering sinners can be reconciled to their Creator. He alone is the gate by which God's sheep can enter his fold. He does not hesitate to call others who pretend to be a gate 'thieves and robbers', stealing the sheep away from their true shepherd. 'I am the way,' he says, 'no one comes to the Father except through me.'

Jesus opened the gate by dying and rising again. Of no one else but him is this true.

OCTOBER 30

'I Am The Resurrection'
John 11:21-26

John gives us a series of breathtaking claims in which Jesus presents himself as the source and giver of eternal life, and as the one through whom the resurrection will happen.

It is Jesus at whose voice the dead will rise to be glorified or condemned (John 5:26-29). It is Jesus who speaks of those who believe as the Father's love-gift to him, and who pledges himself to lose none of them but to raise them all up at the last day (John 6:38-40). And it is Jesus who told Martha, heart-broken at the death of her brother, that whoever lives and believes in him will never die because he is the resurrection and the life (John 11:21-26).

So in the presence of Jesus we are in the presence of God - the eternal Son of the Father, sent by him to be the Saviour of the world, to die to ransom sinners from the power of the grave, to quicken them in spirit by new birth into his kingdom, and, at the last day, to raise them into bodily immortality in the image of himself.

How then can we do other than say, with Thomas, 'My Lord and my God!'

OCTOBER 31

NOVEMBER

WILLIAM STILL

God's
Ultimate
Glory

A Clearing In The Forest
2 Corinthians 4:1,2a

2 Corinthians has been called a 'pathless forest' after the 'laid-out park' of 1 Corinthians. But there are 'clearings' in the forest, offering wonderful things; not least chapters 4 and 5. It is more intensely personal than the first letter, for the apostle bares his soul while waiting for Titus to arrive.

Diverted from Titus, he thinks with triumphant joy of being led in procession by Christ (2:14); and that leads to a profound consideration of the issues of life and death. In turn these lead to discussion of the glory of the New Covenant, and, in chapter 4, to the kind of persons necessary to minister it. The task doesn't daunt Paul whose ministry is by the mercy of God: he 'does not lose heart'. From 4:1 it is clear his trust is not in himself, but in God, whose promises cannot fail, which is a tremendous encouragement to all burdened with a sense of responsibility, for themselves, or for others. Of course, by a radical change in lifestyle, he has renounced shady ways and is open before God, and man - the only true way to live.

'*Truthing It In Love*'
2 Corinthians 4:2-4

The determination to renounce shady ways and come out into the open before God and man has infinite repercussions in our total lifestyle. No deceit in thought, word or deed can be contemplated. Everything in life has to be above-board; as before men, certainly before God. And the very last thing we could consider is any distortion of the Word of God, even in trying to please or attract others. The truth declared plainly, albeit with grace, should appeal to the conscience that this is the very Word of God.

Where consciences are blinded by the god of this world, the gospel is veiled, with little or no understanding of it and its implications. But this must not deflect us or deter us from 'truthing it in love'. Nor do we do this judgmentally (were we not blinded sinners ourselves?) but with compassion for those quite unable to share the light of the glorious gospel of Christ. In fact, pity for blinded souls, like compassion for physically blinded people, will be practical: we will guide them in the truth with accents of profound respect, and win a hearing first of all by our loving attitude.

NOVEMBER 2

True Servants
2 Corinthians 4:5-6

'We do not preach ourselves': this offers us wonderful deliverance from the charge of self-interest, which puts people off. We speak of another, Jesus Christ as Lord, and we but his servants. True servants do not work in their own interests - though they do have interests! - but serve another. The servant does not carry all his Master's burden, only that part of it which applies to his office and service. To approach people, therefore, in this humble, detached and respectful spirit may in many cases evoke at least a respectful response, and perhaps an interested one.

This is what the apostle calls, 'letting our light shine out'. He goes back to creation, when God shone out of the darkness of primeval chaos and said, 'Let there be light!' And since he has caused his light to shine in our hearts, it is the most natural thing in the world that it should shine *out* of them. It is only by deliberately covering up the light with a bowl or bushel of self-interest (Matthew 5:14-15) that it is, alas, hidden from the eyes of those who need to see it.

NOVEMBER 3

The Light
2 Corinthians 4:6

We consider further the nature of the light shining into our hearts that it might shine out to others. It is the light of the knowledge of the glory of God, which cannot mean less than the knowledge of his essential being, whose essence is pure glory.

The glory Saul of Tarsus saw on the Damascus road was an incandescent wonder, sufficient to blind his eyes. It was the glory of One who had trod the earth, fully human with a human face.

That was a great marvel, that the sheer, transcendent effulgence of the eternal God should accommodate itself to a human condition, and shine out, though differently, in his mortal and his resurrection body. But that that light should be given to poor sinners, to shine out of them, is almost too much to take in. Only grace can receive it; but it takes a continual supply of fresh grace to go on believing such gracious and humbling truth, especially against the human odds that would deny it, even those of our own imperfect condition. But he would not command us to 'let our light so shine', if there were no light there to shine.

NOVEMBER 4

Dust And Glory
2 Corinthians 4:7

If Jesus' body was an earthen vessel during his mortal life, what shall we say of our mortal bodies? The precise intention of the Almighty is that his glory should shine from earthen vessels. Thus he breathed into the dust the breath of life and made us of clay, to create us uniquely in his own image. Marvel that he should deliberately take the dust and make it shine with his eternal glory!

But since it was his purpose to exalt, honour and even glorify the dust, its brightness, then, could hardly be attributed to itself, but to his glory, and to his pleasure in thus inhabiting the lowest element of his creation, the dust. This was his kindness to us, not to renounce his glory and yield it to others - he could never do that (see Isaiah 48:11). God must remain God; yet it was his will that the dust of the earth should be exalted to worship him and own the origin of its glory.

Thus he has accorded us the high and holy privilege of being made in his own image and becoming the recipients and the instruments of his glory.

NOVEMBER 5

Not Dismayed
2 Corinthians 4:8-10

We are not only dust, but rebel dust. Our humiliation is double: we are of lowly origin, and culpable into the bargain! This means that having once given ourselves over to God's enemy and ours through the Fall, we are plagued by him as long as we live. And the devil will beset us and take every opportunity to discomfort us.

Yet because the Lord has shone his light into our souls, our enemy will not be allowed to drive us completely into the dark; nor will he ever be allowed to put our light out. For even hunted by persecutors, we will not be forsaken; knocked down by foes, we will not be knocked out.

But how can we, in many times and ways, be near disaster, yet never overtaken by it? Ah! the light which shines in us is a light which came to its brightness through the greatest darkness of all, the dying of the Lord Jesus. But he rose again; and so, by sharing his death and resurrection, despite every adversity and harassment, we are not dismayed, because our suffering is under divine control, and can never get out of hand. We shall rise again, as he rose. What a comfort!

NOVEMBER 6

All For Us

2 Corinthians 4:10

The Lord Jesus' dying was all for us and on our behalf; he died our death to sin and Satan. And he died it, because we sinners could not safely die that death ourselves - we would have gone down into a lost eternity. It is only in his dying for us - and you might say he was a long time a-dying, namely all the three years of his costly ministry - that we may safely die the death to sin, self and Satan and emerge triumphant, as this verse says.

This is the evidence of truly Christian lives that, always on the point of giving up or giving in, we never do, but escape from disasters galore and survive and recover in most amazing ways. It may seem a hazardous way to live; but it was the life our Lord lived: should not his servants tread it still? After all, there is the excitement of danger, and yet the assurance that all is under the control of the principle and power which brought Christ himself through his awful death into resurrection power and glory. It worked for him (although all he went through was for our sakes); it must work for us, for it was done *for* us.

NOVEMBER 7

Many Deaths
2 Corinthians 4:11

Notice the 'always' here as in verse 10. This is the nature of the death/life which those who are fully committed to Christ must inevitably lead. We are being delivered, or handed over, to death in the midst of life, on account of Jesus. This was the way he lived, his cross being simply the climax of a life of 'dyings', with every death followed by its appropriate resurrection.

We, therefore, are to follow him, at a distance of course in every sense; and by his Holy Spirit enter into the fruit of both his dying and rising. Our life, like his in a hostile world, must encompass many deaths ('deaths oft', Paul says, in chapter 11:23, but see the whole passage from verse 21ff); and such a life must necessarily emerge from these various 'deaths', often miraculously, into many multi-varied resurrections. Not only so, but these miraculous deliverances are plain for all to see; for it is in our mortal flesh that they are seen for what they are, namely amazing providences of God.

They say the cat has nine lives. The Christian, leaning hard on his Lord and enduring for his sake, has many more.

NOVEMBER 8

The Death To Self
2 Corinthians 4:12

There is a major change here: Paul in his assessment
of his ministry and witness has been thinking thus far
of the effect on himself of sharing Christ's death and
resurrection; but at verse 12 he drives the thought of
verses 10 and 11 outwards to others. For the death of
Jesus Christ applied to our lives not only leads to daily
miraculous resurrections for us, but should also ex-
tend to those we are seeking to serve.

So we die, not only with the prospect of enjoying
our own personal resurrections, but also those which
others shall enjoy through our deaths on their behalf;
because our dying is naturally geared to God's will in
respect of our ministry to them, as well as to ourselves.
We die to live for them as well as for ourselves.

This dual benefit, then, is therefore wonderfully
fruitful and manifold; for two distinct effects are
being wrought by our willingness to die the death to
self in Christ: Christian character is being produced in
us as his death does its gracious work; and because the
quality of our ministry is affected by this, others are
being brought progressively to the feet of Christ.

Clinging To Faith
2 Corinthians 4:13,14

Paul is so sure of these things concerning our death and resurrection in Christ, which in their practical mystery he has expounded wonderfully, that he has to speak of them and unfold them for the edification of others. He is reminded of the words the Psalmist uttered in a time of trouble, asking for his soul to be delivered from death, his eyes from tears, his feet from stumbling, and that he might walk in the land of the living. He said, 'I clung to my faith, even when I said, faith cannot be shaken'; or as the Good News version has it, 'I kept on believing, even when I said, "I am completely crushed".' Or, as the Berkeley version has it, 'I clung to my faith, even when I said, I am sorely afflicted' (Psalm 116:10).

It is the same faith as the Psalmist had, but the Apostle can declare it with new conviction because of the resurrection of Jesus from the dead; for he is sure that the God who brought the Lord Jesus from the dead will also raise and bring him, with all the saints, into his presence.

God's Ultimate Glory

2 Corinthians 4:15

This speaking out to the Corinthians the profoundest things of the gospel, from a heart full of conviction, is entirely in their interests and for their benefit. For thereby grace is reaching more and more, and therefore thanksgiving for divine mercy and goodness is overflowing to the glory of God. This outreach is of the essence of the work of God, and Paul takes every aspect of it and every stage of its progress into consideration and sees it through to its ultimate end, namely the glory of God.

It is important for us not to foreshorten our view of what is being done in the Lord's service. We must not intercept its eventual goals; for that would concede a diminution of their full achievement and glory. In our work for the Lord we must always see through to God's ultimate glory, and that will prevent us from getting bogged down in personal preoccupations and thinking more of ourselves and of our life and service than is warranted. We must always refer back to God so that all we think, say and do may be properly oriented to him.

Through Thick And Thin
2 Corinthians 4:16

The result of Paul's radical view of the Lord's work means that we will never lose heart. Why should we lose heart? Because outwardly there seems to be cause for it. The NIV says, 'Though outwardly we are wasting away'; but the original says, '*If indeed* the outward man is being disabled', which suggests an *appearance* of being disabled; or there may be a temporary disability, which inclines us to think so, but is a lie of the devil.

The truth is that whatever may appear to the contrary, we are being renewed day by day, so that we keep going on, through thick and thin. And while emotionally we may be inclined to whimper and cry out that we are wasting away, the truth may be the very opposite, which is being hid from our eyes by the enemy splashing eye-wash on our faces.

There are three who may be consulted concerning our condition: ourselves, who are poor guides; the devil who loves to dupe and daunt us and is a liar; and the Lord, who knows all. He says we are being renewed day by day. Fair enough!

NOVEMBER 12

Light Afflictions
2 Corinthians 4:17

So present afflictions are light! Whose opinion is this? The Lord, by his apostle. They should know! If the apostle - not to say our Lord - had not suffered, we might ignore him, but what is the truth? See our Lord in Gethsemane and on the Cross, and Paul in 2 Corinthians 12.

But on what ground does Paul make this seemingly depreciatory comment on our troubles? On the ground of comparing them with what they are accomplishing. He is not depreciating them; he is too sensitive and sympathetic to do that. He is simply saying that for all their comparative lightness, they are accomplishing an eternal weight of glory, which must mean that in real terms, there is practically no comparison. So he is not making little or light of our troubles, but is simply saying that, sore as they are, they are as nothing compared with what they are producing, namely something so weighty as to belong to eternal glory, the ultimate essence.

'But,' we may say, 'These two, our present troubles and future glory seem so unequal now.' Yes, but then the mind that Christ gives us lives realistically, in both worlds.

NOVEMBER 13

The Most Solid Comfort
2 Corinthians 4:18

We said yesterday that the mind of Christ lives realistically in both the present world and in that which is to come. But our verse says we are nonetheless to fix our eyes on that future world, not this present world. It is not absolute, of course, for we live in this world; yet our forward-looking eyes should be set on that one.

But always? Are we to live, permanently, in the future? No, that would be to forget what this theme is about. It is about the effectual antidote to suffering: that, in distress, we look away, not only to what is to be, but to what that 'to be' is producing now, by present suffering. For the difference between the two worlds is simply that this one is temporal and temporary; that one, for ever. But, for all its everlastingness to come, it is still future, whereas this one is now painfully with us.

The most solid comfort, therefore, in time of trouble, is to hold on, not only to what is to be, but to do so realising that the future will depend for its quality on how we hold on, now!

A Heavenly Shelter
2 Corinthians 5:1-4

Paul now turns to questions of the hereafter. In view of the temporality of this present mortal life, fully stated in the preceding chapter, our earthly life is aptly described as a tent, which for pilgrims is a temporary dwelling-place. For it to be taken down and destroyed is not great disaster when we have another dwelling from God, not made of this world's transient material, but eternal in the heavens.

In this tent we may well groan, as the children of Israel did in the wildernesses between Egypt and Canaan. But what is this groan? It is about our tent of mortal flesh being taken down, lest we be bereft of cover to our naked souls. Ah, the tent is now the clothing of flesh. What a delicious mixture of metaphors! The groaning is therefore lest we be found naked between death and resurrection. Not so; Calvin says that those who are clothed with the righteousness of Christ pass on after death to the shelter of heaven, and Tasker believes Paul is underlining his certainty that a heavenly shelter awaits him immediately upon death. But we will not receive a resurrection body, until Christ comes.

NOVEMBER 15

Over-clothed

2 Corinthians 5:4

Verse 4 presents an arresting thought. Paul says he does not want to be unclothed of his mortal body by death. He sees his life as more than merely in the body. Rather, by Christ's coming, he hopes to be clothed with his heavenly dwelling (still mixing his metaphors!).

This is read by Paul Barnett as a wish to be 'over-clothed'. He says when we change clothes we do not put on the new until we have put off the old, but here the apostle is hoping that Christ will come and put on the new clothes of his resurrection body over the top of the old, so that death will be overtaken, and its very possibility swallowed up by resurrection life.

But even if death should precede Christ's coming, he would hope not to be found naked, for having been clothed with the righteousness of Christ, the lack of his resurrection body would not leave him without shelter. He has a house in heaven from God, an eternal house, not made with hands. Either way he is safe and secure, but he would prefer the Lord's coming to death. This was not granted.

NOVEMBER 16

The Deposit
2 Corinthians 5:5

These things would never have occurred, even to the apostle, if God had not purposed them and made them known to him. Indeed, the Lord made us for this; he is simply working out his long-term purpose, and in the meantime has given us his Holy Spirit as the deposit which guarantees this very thing. Paul expands on this in Ephesians 1:14, where he says that believers have been sealed by the Holy Spirit 'who is a deposit guaranteeing our inheritance until the redemption of those who are [already] God's possession'.

The word 'deposit' may be translated 'pledge', 'guarantee', 'first instalment' (an expression common in hire-purchase), or 'arles' (the deposit made to fish workers to commence the East Anglian herring season as earnest of full wages to come).

To speak of the Holy Spirit as an 'earnest' of our inheritance to come, does not imply that the divine deposit is less than the fullness of the Holy Spirit. He does not come to depart, to be wooed back in a second experience of grace. He is present in fullness by the new birth, or not at all.

Never Alone
2 Corinthians 5:6-8

The good cheer, or courage, or confidence the apostle speaks of here is on account of the presence of the Holy Spirit, referred to yesterday, in the life of the saint - never alone! The promises, in Deuteronomy 31:6 and Hebrews 13:5, that the Lord will never leave us nor forsake us has its fullest meaning in the indwelling presence of the Spirit of God. It is that assurance which makes life 'away from the Lord', because we are 'at home in the body', at least bearable! We live by faith, not by sight; and so, although it is obviously better to be at home with the Lord, as we shall be one day, than to be away from him because we are still in the body, we bear it and make the best of it by his aid.

It is this fact which creates the tension within us between the two worlds. The legitimate pleasures which this world affords compete with the trials to which flesh is heir in this present evil world. This is because the Lord is with us constantly helping us make the best of the 'bad job' we have made, thanks to Adam, by letting Satan and sin into our lives.

NOVEMBER 18

In His Will

2 Corinthians 5:9

The aim of our lives, since we were born, and born again of God's will, is to please him; whether in the body, and therefore in a manner of speaking away from the Lord, or not. It is obvious that what he wants for us at present is to be in the body, with all trials tinctured by his grace; for he could take our breath away in a moment if he chose.

So we live, not by our own will, which he is training us to blend more and more completely with his, but rejoicing in the glow of the grace of his revealed will, since anything else would be pain, whatever fleeting pleasure we gained by it meantime. For our chief pleasure must be in his will, even when that will denies our carnal desires; for to be in anything contrary to his will can hardly be pleasure to the true child of God!

It is in his will, and in that alone, that we have his peace. The reason for this is clear: our highest pleasure as social beings is in fellowship, especially fellowship with the saints, but supremely with God himself.

NOVEMBER 19

Reward Or Loss

2 Corinthians 5:10

We spoke yesterday of the pleasure of living according to the divine will, and therefore in a condition of peace with our Lord. For to be against his will not only detracts from legitimate pleasure, but incurs his judgment upon ourselves.

It is not a punishing judgment which separates from God, since we have already read that nothing shall separate us from him, because we are committed to him, and as such are bound to him by ties, not only of creation and redemption, but of the superior tie of filial love. It is therefore in love that he chastises his own now, lest coming before his judgment seat with a load of sins committed after we become his, we suffer, in the words of 1 Corinthians 3:15, loss.

Now loss in heaven very likely means loss of reward. This is seldom taught, so that to many it seems like an alien doctrine, and certainly a painful one as many speakers have proved! All deeds are wiped away by Jesus' blood as to punishment, but our deeds as Christians will be judged, for reward or loss, at Christ's judgment seat.

NOVEMBER 20

A Godly Fear
2 Corinthians 5:11

This complex fear is mingled with the love which the apostle has found in God through Christ - a godly fear lest he should displease the Lord who gave him such confidence concerning his destiny.

In respect of those to whom he longs to tell the story of salvation, this fear consists largely of the terror which struck at his heart on the Damascus road when he was suddenly confronted with the ascended Christ in glory. The elements of that fear remain because of the reality of eternal punishment for those finally refusing the Lord. This is the dread which impels him to implore men to make their peace with God, lest at the last they find themselves, negatively, out of God's love and plunged into outer darkness, and, positively, missing all the richness of God's salvation.

Paul is eager in the sight of the all-knowing God to tell men the true state of affairs between God and man; and having done so to the Corinthians, he hopes their consciences may have been struck with the reality of what he says.

This needs to be our zealous aim also, living in the light of these realities.

NOVEMBER 21

False Piety
2 Corinthians 5:12

The apostle dares to be fiercely personal in warning the Corinthians of the danger of incurring eternal wrath. He now explains that, contrary to what they might suppose, he is not trying to impress them with his own zeal. Unfortunately, a letter affords no additional support by way of vocal inflection or facial expression. Nonetheless he hoped that his zeal would encourage those of right mind to support him in respect of detractors who would pull him down.

Paul's detractors were those who, not sharing his deep thoughts on the solemnities of judgment or, doubtless, other deep things, were trying to put a brave and impressive face on it and appearing to be, as such people do, more pious than the pious.

Paul writes beautifully and searchingly of false piety in Colossians 2:16-23. There he is thinking of meticulous observance of externals, which (17) are a shadow of things to come, whereas the substance - the body - is Christ himself. It is easy to be impressed with what the apostle calls 'an appearance of wisdom, self-imposed worship, false humility and harsh treatment of the body, but lacking any value in restraining sensual indulgence' (Colossians 2:23).

NOVEMBER 22

Constrained By Christ's Love
2 Corinthians 5:13-15

Paul seems to be trying hard to present his case as if he were standing before them, with the signs his presence would afford of what he was saying. After all, he will later tell of extraordinary experiences (12:1-4). Although speaking in tongues more than all of them, he possibly never did so in fellowship (1 Corinthians 14:18-19); nonetheless, he must have experienced sufficient manifestations of the Spirit while amongst them for his critics to suggest that he took mad turns!

No, he says, these experiences, although you were aware of them, were not for you, but for God. It is what I say in all soberness of spirit which you have to take heed of; for when I visibly hold myself in when the Holy Spirit is powerfully upon me, I am simply constrained by the love of Christ to exercise a ministry which will be enlightening and beneficial to you.

And that love has its ground in Christ's death, because he died for all, for all were dead in trespasses and sins. He died for them, and calls them to follow him into that death which leads to new, self-giving life (15).

NOVEMBER 23

A New Creation

2 Corinthians 5:15-17

The fact that One died for all indicates the universality of sin; Christ's purpose being that those he died for should live another life than their former selfish inturned life, which was a kind of death, and would lead to endless death. Rather, they should live the life procured for them by his death and resurrection. And that life, although necessarily lived in the old, mortal body until death, is nonetheless as radically different from the former life as will be the destiny of the new, compared with the destiny of the old. This is declared in verse 17 in the terms that have been compared with the Copernican revolution: that if anyone is in Christ, he is a new creation, the old life is passed away, the new has come to pass.

Perhaps the categorical nature of verse 17 helps us to understand the complexity of verse 16, which seems to mean that we now regard our humanity as so bound up with Christ's that we see its mortality in the light of his greater, fuller life. That is a life which is presently inherent in the life of the believer, but its full glory will not be seen until we are glorified by the coming of Christ.

NOVEMBER 24

Friends With God

2 Corinthians 5:18

Our total newness is from God. The new life set before us is so sovereignly authoritative that there is a stamp on it which leaves any sacrifice we have to make a small price to pay. Indeed, it is all gain, for we are reconciled to our Maker by his Son, Jesus Christ - friends with God! Is that not fabulous enough to take our breath away and leave us gasping for want of an orientation to match it, or compare it with? One of the greatest things that could be said of Abraham was that he was a 'friend of God' (2 Chronicles 20:7; Isaiah 41:8; James 2:23).

But friends of God, like growing youngsters in the home, are required to assume responsibility for their advantages. The children of God, as soon as it has dawned on them how wonderfully reconciled to God they are by becoming his friends, are given the ministry of reconciliation. And see how reasonable that is. Surely the least we can do for him who has so blessed us is to share his good news with others: that God is more than willing to be friends with us on his most costly and generous terms.

NOVEMBER 25

God Was In Christ
2 Corinthians 5:19a

And this is the ministry of reconciliation we are to offer to others when the full glory of its message has dawned upon our own souls: *that God was in Christ*! Christ was no mere man working and suffering for God, but the Father was with him and in him, working his holy will to reconcile the world to himself through his sacrifice. Furthermore, this reconciliation not only includes that of the Lord's own children for whom he died, but also the natural universe, drawn into the Fall by Adam's sin, as Romans 8:20-22 tells us.

But what does this involve for the Father and the Son? All our trespasses have to be accounted for and dealt with, and since James 2:10 tells us that nothing but 100% perfection is required for acceptance with God, our Lord must attain that degree of satisfaction on our behalf before the Father safely and soundly imputes them all to him. However, David foresaw this in Psalm 32:1-2, when he prophesied, 'Blessed is he whose transgressions are forgiven, whose sins are covered. Blessed is the man whose sin the Lord does not count against him and in whose spirit is no deceit'.

NOVEMBER 26

Christ's Ambassadors
2 Corinthians 5:19b-20

This ministry of reconciliation has been committed to us, so that we become Christ's ambassadors. Now, an ambassador is the representative of his country and government in a foreign land. We are called upon to be ambassadors for Christ in this alien world of lost humanity, to bring the friendship of none other than our Maker and heavenly Father to bear on their forlorn and lost souls. They may have nothing but the haziest notions of the heavenly experience which could be theirs if they understood and accepted that we are speaking in God's name and on behalf of his Son Jesus Christ, pleading with them to be reconciled to God. Indeed, we are under commission to do so, for our risen Lord, before he left the earth, said to his disciples, 'All authority in heaven and on earth has been given to me. Therefore go and make disciples of all nations...'

Perhaps the dignity of our calling has not struck us before, because such a ministry of reconciliation has to be conducted in the homeliest fashion, if there is any hope of influencing people in a world as cynical about the faith as ours has become.

NOVEMBER 27

Made Sin
2 Corinthians 5:21a

This is one of the great verses in the New Testament, and contains worlds of meaning.

But the first part of the statement is so stark that many scholars have sought to make some accommodation to the shocking import that Christ was made sin for us; and some have simply not believed it. But that is no way to treat the Word of God.

The nearest to this startling statement elsewhere in the New Testament is found in Galatians 3:13, where Paul says Christ was 'made a curse for us'. But 'to be made sin' seems on the face of it an impossibility if we are speaking of the sinless Saviour who challenged men, 'Which of you convinces me of sin?'

However, the order of the words in the original really obviates a great deal of fearful argument, because the Greek begins, 'The One not knowing sin, on our behalf, God made sin.' This reads awkwardly, but here the truth is more important than beauty or elegance, and the original order encourages us to seek to understand what 'being made sin' can possibly mean in the light of the overruling statement of our Lord's sinlessness.

NOVEMBER 28

This Is Marvellous!
2 Corinthians 5:21b

To continue with yesterday's thought, only a sinless man could be 'made sin' for others, since otherwise he would be condemned for his own sin and therefore could do nothing for others. If he sinned (according to James' perfect standard, which is that 'whosoever stumbles in one point is guilty of all', 2:10), he would die for that sin and be lost. He could only bear the penalty of the sins of others fully, and on the third day rise from the dead uncondemned, if he had no sin of his own to keep him down. And we know from Peter's words at Pentecost in Acts 2:24, that 'death could not keep its hold on him'.

This is marvellous! Where, then, have our sins gone with their dire everlasting penalty? They cease to exist so that if in heaven we were to approach the throne of the Lamb and enquire about our sinful past, the Lord himself would have forgotten it all. If *we* are to remember them, hereafter, it seems likely that the Lord will have forgotten all about them, having, as someone has put it, 'cast them into the sea of his forgetfulness'.

NOVEMBER 29

The Righteousness Of God

2 Corinthians 5:21c

So far we have been looking at the negative side. Why did it all happen? That we should be 'made the righteousness of God in him'. So here is another startling thing: if Christ was 'made sin, who knew no sin', that means that he was the object of the wrath of God for the sins of the saints. As I once daringly put it: he was God's 'Criminal'! What, then, do *we* become? The text here does not say, either that righteousness is imputed to us, which it is; or that it is imparted to us in the full and perfect sense, which it is not yet, since we still sin! But Christ was 'made sin' that we might *become* 'the righteousness of God in him'. He, the sinless One, is made sin; we the sinful ones, are made righteousness, in him.

Isn't that staggering? Talk about a daring but fully justified exchange (see Romans 3:26)! Think of it along with John Wesley translating Nicolaus Ludwig von Zinzendorf:

> Jesus, Thy blood and righteousness
> My beauty are, my glorious dress;
> Midst flaming worlds with these arrayed,
> With joy shall I lift up my head.

NOVEMBER 30

DECEMBER

CONNIE DEVER

*God's Words
And Ours*

God's Powerful Words

Let all the earth fear the LORD; let all the people of the world revere him. For he spoke, and it came to be; he commanded, and it stood firm (Psalm 33:8-9).

Many a tyrant has prided himself in being so feared by his subjects that his smallest request sends them scrambling to fulfil it. His words have power over them because they are backed by forces ready to punish. He is someone to fear. But shortly, that man's kingdom falls to another and his words lose their ability to fulfil his desires. Now the new king holds that power.

But our God is different. His words are ever powerful and ever to be feared. He does not even need the arms and legs of servants to see that his words are fulfilled. Clothed with his omnipotence they are able to do whatever he wills. And never will there be someone new to usurp his power. No. 'He commanded, and it stood firm.'

Such a God as this deserves a different kind of fear - our reverent worship and willing obedience. We, too, should hasten to do his will. But we have the wonderful position of serving not a tyrant, but the loving, gracious Lord.

DECEMBER 1

God's Trustworthy Words

He humbled you, causing you to hunger and then feeding you with manna . . . to teach you that man does not live on bread alone but on every word that comes from the mouth of the LORD (Deuteronomy 8:3).

A lesson in humility would seem to be the last lesson former slaves would need. Yet it was the first lesson the LORD taught Israel upon leaving Egypt. If humility means to think lowly of oneself, then slavery had taught them that. But the LORD had true humility in mind: that humility which acknowledges complete dependence upon God and shows itself in willing obedience to him. So he led them repeatedly into impossible situations and then rescued them. Only with this lesson learned, could Israel please God and enjoy his blessings.

We, too, have the needful, but joyful, task of learning godly humility. It is needful, for God's children can only survive by obedience to his words. Especially so when, like Israel, we are asked to trust God in circumstances beyond our understanding. And it is joyful, because we know that crossing seas on dry land and manna from heaven characterise this One whose word we are humbly to trust and obey.

DECEMBER 2

God's Comforting Words

My soul is weary with sorrow; strengthen me according to your word (Psalm 119:28).

Something has happened; someone has gone. There is no undoing or bringing back. And we are left consumed with the sorrow of it all. There's the shock, the pain, then an emptiness that lingers on. And our soul feels like crumbling under the strain. Such is the Psalmist's experience. The English translation masks the turmoil expressed in the Hebrew: 'I have collapsed with intense sorrow,' is a clearer rendering.

Comfort and strength for one so sorrowful is elusive. Yet it can be found in the word of God. Not an easy comfort of complete answers nor an immediate remedy for the pain and loneliness, but a truly solid comfort, nonetheless.

It brings the comforting knowledge that the God who lovingly gave up his Son for us, is he who has carefully chosen the way for our life. And, with his unfailing power, he promises to make all our life's events work for good, and to give us strength to make it through the process - even through deepest heartache. Here the sorrowful may go for lasting consolation. For only God's words are so rich with unchangeable power, truth and love.

DECEMBER 3

God's True Words

For the word of the LORD is right and true; he is
faithful in all he does (Psalm 33:4).

'There are no absolutes, only possibilities,' claims
this world. Truth is replaced with 'You can't be certain,' right with 'do what's best for you,' and faithfulness with 'I want to keep my options open.' But when
absolutes are discarded to gain a freer life, insecurity,
meaninglessness, and despair arise instead.

The word of God stands in stark contrast to this
philosophy. It proclaims itself to be the right and true
words of One of unending faithfulness. Those yoked
to it do have to refuse some of the world's delicacies,
but they are the recipients of peace, fulfilment and
hope.

Yet sometimes even we believers treat his word as
unreliable. We downplay its absolute truthfulness,
when its advice is uncomfortable. And we worry
about the needs it has promised to provide. But even
here there is comfort. Though we struggle with our
lack of faith in him, he will never give us cause to
struggle with a lack of his faithfulness. He is always
as good as his word. Therefore let us strive to live out
with confidence what we know to be true and trust-
worthy.

DECEMBER 4

God's Successful Word

[My word] will not return to me empty, but will accomplish what I desire and achieve the purpose for which I sent it (Isaiah 55:11).

God's word knows no impossible mission. It is that servant of God which is able to do all that he desires. There is not even a possibility of failure.

We are called to be God's servants, too. But we do not fare so well. Many times we know what God wants to achieve through us, but out of selfishness or weakness we do not do it. Realising the sad state of our affairs, we should not wallow about, but should seek out a remedy. Where selfishness thwarts God's purposes, we should confess it, turn from it, and ask God to make us more self-forgetful. Where weakness exists, let us not become discouraged. For we are God's workmanship, and his work is to see Christ made in us.

And who is it that God has sent to accomplish this impossible task? His word, which works with unfailing ability. Give thanks to him for his gracious work in us and his powerful word which does in us with ease what we desire but could never do on our own.

DECEMBER 5

God's Cutting Word

For the Word of God is living and active. Sharper than any double-edged sword, it penetrates even to dividing soul and spirit, joints and marrow; it judges the thoughts and attitudes of the heart (Hebrews 4:12).

Knives that deftly separate body tissues most naturally conjure up images of medieval sword-play or surgical procedures. Shocking as it is, this is a description of God's words at work in us. For the Lord employs his word in our lives as both a soldier's sword and a surgeon's scalpel. His battle cry is, 'Be holy, because I am holy.' His word confronts the enemy - sin - it finds in us. That which was rightly the king's has become enemy territory and his word has come to reclaim it. Then, with a scalpel's precision, his word searches for and removes our hearts' malignancies, no matter how hidden.

The word of God is active in us, but we must play our part, too. By frequently meditating on God's word, we can surround the enemy with the king's troops. And by obeying what we read, we make ourselves quiet patients during surgery. A surrounded enemy is most easily conquered, and a submissive patient, most quickly healed.

DECEMBER 6

God's Enlightening Word

Your word is a lamp to my feet and a light for my path (Psalm 119:105).

An evening stroll in the Psalmist's Israel, three thousand years ago, could be hazardous. When the sun set, darkness reigned. There were no street lights to temper it. And the paths were not the smooth pavements we know. Many of them were far from level, with rocks and brush scattered about them to ambush the unwary traveller. A small oil lamp was a person's only aid. Its little flame gave its grateful bearer just enough light to make safe his next few steps. Without it, he would certainly stumble.

It is God's word that guides us on the path of our life: 'Your word is a *lamp* to my *feet*.' We must not expect a street light that shows up large sections of path. It is like an oil lamp that sheds just enough light to help us manoeuvre around our next few bumpy steps. It is for *my* path. His word will give *me* the specific help *I* need for the particular plan he has for *me*. We should study and memorise his words so that we carry his Lamp with us always to enlighten our paths.

DECEMBER 7

Our Words: Intended To Please God

May the words of my mouth and the meditation of my heart be pleasing in your sight, O LORD (Psalm 19:14)

When people are convinced of God's presence, everything around them testifies to God's glory. And when they are convinced that the Bible is God's word, everything inside them desires to be conformed to it. David's plea in Psalm 19 for a pleasing heart and mouth is borne out of such convictions.

First he admires the vast splendour of the heavens. He is amazed at their ability, though only speechless objects, to proclaim universally their Creator's glory. David's thoughts pivot here and turn towards God's written proclamations. God's Word reflects him by its trustworthiness, righteousness and perfection. And its life-giving instruction is all-sufficient for the believer's needs.

And then David's thoughts turn towards himself. The skies have no mouth yet they proclaim God's glory. What does his more able tongue proclaim? He has God's Word from which to learn; has his heart responded to its instruction? Aware of his failures, he asks forgiveness and utters his half-prayer, half-resolution: 'May my words and thoughts please you, O LORD!'

DECEMBER 8

Our Words: Called To Forgive

Forgive whatever grievances you may have against one another.   Forgive as the Lord forgave you (Colossians 3:13).

'I forgive you.' Those are God's pardoning words to us, his offenders. Without them, we would not have eternal life or know Christ's peace, joy and love. Instead, we would remain in the bondage of despair, with the guilt of our offences and the insecurity of feeling unlovable. Forgiveness is God's greatest gift to us, because he gave us what we needed most, deserved least and were unable to obtain ourselves. It is also his costliest because it was obtained by his Son's death.

'I forgive you.' Those are the pardoning words that Paul tells us to use with our offenders. We must release our heart's prisoners. They must not remain in the bondage of our resentment, with the guilt of their offences, and feeling the insecurity of our withheld love. Forgiveness is our greatest gift to them, because it is what they need most, deserve least and are most unable to obtain. It is also very costly, because it means we must silence our heart's wounds that want to accuse and harm.

Lord, fills us with your boundless love, so we can obey this most Christ-like of commands.

DECEMBER 9

Our Words: Intended To Give Thanks

Give thanks to the LORD, for he is good. His love endures forever (Psalm 136:1)

Psalm 136 prompted Israel to remember why they should thank the LORD. For although he was King of all kings and Creator of all the earth, yet he chose them as his special possession. He freed them from slavery and then sustained them in the desert with food from his own hand. He subdued great kings to give them a promised land. They were often doubtful and faithless, but the LORD treated them with unfailing loyalty.

If Israel had reason to be thankful, surely we, the new Israel, have even more. The LORD is our King and Creator, but also Father and Friend. He has freed us from an even greater bondage: spiritual bondage. He filled their stomachs in a provision-less desert, yet he has filled our spirits with his Holy Spirit. And though he subdued earthly princes to give them the Promised Land, for us he subdued the Prince of darkness and gave us the Kingdom of heaven in our hearts.

Since our blessings are greater, so should be our thanksgiving. Our earthly treasures may fluctuate, but we can always give thanks for these greater, everlasting blessings. May our eternal blessings be met with eternal thanksgiving!

DECEMBER 10

Our Words: Intended To Be Patient

A patient man has great understanding, but a quick-tempered man displays folly (Proverbs 14:29).

The person who can control his tongue in anger-provoking situations is set apart from his hasty-tempered counterpart by two qualities. First, he has 'great understanding'. He realises that rage does not resolve anything but only multiplies trouble and grief. He advocates James' advice to 'be quick to listen, slow to speak, and slow to get angry.' And he desires that his reactions should reflect 'the wisdom that comes from heaven [which] 'is first of all pure; then peace-loving, considerate, submissive, full of mercy and good fruit, impartial and sincere' (James 3:17).

But for his actions actually to reflect his understanding, he needs the second quality - patience. It is pat-ience that stills the tongue long enough for understanding instead of passion to shape its words. This second quality is hardest acquired because it is not a concept for our minds to grasp, but a fruit of the Spirit's work in us. It comes only gradually, as the Spirit cultivates our hearts and makes them fertile under his hand.

Lord, fill our minds with your wisdom and our hearts with your Spirit, that we might live the righteous lives you desire!

DECEMBER 11

Our Words: Not Intended For Gossip

The words of a gossip are like choice morsels; they go down to a man's inmost parts (Proverbs 18:8).

Gossips are people who like to see what is interesting in others without looking to the interests of others. They spread others' delicate matters with disregard to the injury it may cause. Many different 'caterers' serve gossip's 'choice morsels'. Boredom or curiosity lead some people to gossip. Others seek to fill nervous silences or to make themselves feel important. Many tattle about someone else's wrong-doing because they are too timid to confront the wrong-doer himself about it. And there are those who feel such hatred towards others that they deliberately spread malicious rumours to ruin them.

No matter what the reason, gossip's tasty titbits have the same effect on the listeners. The gossip goes down to their 'inmost parts', poisoning thoughts and actions. Prejudices form, animosity is aroused and unity is broken, all because of an indiscreet tongue! We can avoid being poison-spreaders by not speaking or listening to gossip. And we can prevent its occurrence in the first place by settling our disputes with others quickly and directly. So that the only thing left for gossips to tell is our unwillingness to gossip!

DECEMBER 12

Our Words: Intended For The Gospel

So the man went away and began to tell in the Decapolis how much Jesus had done for him. And all the people were amazed... (Mark 5:20).

After Jesus had freed the man of Gadara from demon-possession, he entrusted him with a task. Jesus himself would not be travelling further into the Decapolis. The countryside was in uproar over the drowned pigs. They pleaded for Jesus to leave and he complied. But the healed Gadarene man went, by Jesus' orders, as his witness. Jesus told him to tell his family what happened. He did; but apparently his joy was too great to be satisfied with that small audience. He spread his story to people in the entire region. And as he spoke, people responded.

Jesus sends us out as witnesses also - all of us. Not just extroverts, or those with exciting conversion stories, or those gifted in answering tough questions. Those people may have special opportunities, but not all the opportunities. All of us need to share our own conversion story.

Let it not be from our lips' hesitancy that others do not hear about Jesus. May we remember the matchless joy of our salvation and overflow with testimony to it.

DECEMBER 13

Our Words: Intended To Be Loyal

In all this, Job did not sin in what he said (Job 2:10).

The contest was set, and a word would win it. The LORD held up Job as one who truly feared him. Satan wagered that Job's loyalty to God was only based on God's blessings, not on loyalty to God himself. Replace good things with bad and Job would curse God. The LORD allowed the contest. Job's words would indicate whose opinion was justified.

Job's life collapsed before him as he was stripped of relatives, friends, fortune, and health. Satan used Job's wife to provoke him: 'Curse God and die!' she said. But the LORD knew his man. Job's heart was loyal to God and he rebutted the temptress: 'Shall we accept good from God, and not trouble?' Job was confused as to why this was happening to him, but he was never confused as to where his loyalty lay. God's consideration was right. Not even once did he sin with his words, let alone curse God.

Wherein lies the loyalty of our hearts - to God or to his gifts? When we are 'under consideration' may our words, like Job's, prove God right in esteeming us truly loyal to him.

DECEMBER 14

Our Words: Powerful To Influence

Reckless words pierce like a sword, but the tongue of the wise brings healing (Proverbs 12:18).

It is hard to avoid the damage done by deliberately cruel words. But this verse in Proverbs points out that thoughtless words, though they may slide from our mouths innocently and slip by quietly, may also deeply wound. Words are such a natural part of our lives. We use them for everything from asking for postage stamps to sharing our deepest secrets. And because they are so commonplace, it can become easy to forget the powerful impact they can have on others.

To avoid as many unintentional hurts as possible, we must make choosing words a conscious effort. We must consider the recipients of our words: what are their needs, fears, weaknesses? What would help or encourage them? And remember, the Lord's ear is upon our conversation: would these words please him? The answers to these questions help us decide what to say and how to say it. When we do this, we are like the wise who store up knowledge (Proverbs 10:14), and then let their hearts guide their mouths (Proverbs 16:23). And our words will bring healing because they have the listeners' benefit in mind.

DECEMBER 15

Our Words: Intended To Be Truthful

Better is open rebuke than hidden love (Proverbs 27:5).

'The truth though sometimes daunting, is always good to know,' said Thomas Winning. And a friend who will be frank with us is a rare treasure. There are sinful things about us that we cannot see or do not want to see. We need friends who will confront us with these things. Many friends are unwilling to speak truthfully out of fear of hurting or displeasing each other. But that friend who will speak out shows he cares more for our benefit than even the pleasure of our company.

Frankness *is* a great divider of friendships. Not that it splits up friends, but that it divides acquaintances from true friendships. Were we to assess our relationships how would they fare? Perhaps more than we would like fall on the wrong side of the dividing line. Fortunately, honesty is born more out of training than talent. We can coax each other out of what the verse calls 'hidden love' - that is, love that conceals the needed truth - and encourage openness with each other. For even though correction is hard to hear from anyone, it is more palatable from a kind friend than from anyone else.

DECEMBER 16

Our Words: Not Intended For Grumbling

> If only we had died by the LORD's hand in Egypt! There we sat round pots of meat ... but you have brought us out into this desert to starve (Exodus 16:3).

The Israelites wondered how their grand deliverance from Egypt could have ended in the wilderness with parched mouths and rumbling stomachs. They reviewed the past weeks for answers. They could have taken encouragement from the numerous miraculous events that had occurred. But they wanted to grumble, so they saw only what would make them feel mistreated. They saw no mud-pits, but only meat-pots. Moses and Aaron were not Israel's deliverers, but deceivers plotting her ruin. And the LORD? Slaying them in Egypt would have been better than this rescue!

Israel's grumbling revealed an ungrateful, slanderous attitude towards God. Eventually, it led to punishment. What happened to the grumbling Israelites should be a warning to us (I Corinthians 10:10-11). Grumbling about our problems seriously offends God. Instead, God would have us cast our cares on him, recall his past unfailing care for us, and be thankful for any blessings we presently enjoy. And, when nothing earthly comforts us, we must dwell on heaven, where there will be no more trials about which to grumble!

DECEMBER 17

Jesus: God's Incarnate Word

The Word became flesh and made his dwelling among us (John 1:14).

Loving-kindness characterised the Lord's relationship with Israel, but it was loving-kindness from a distance. The Israelites' sin prohibited them from entering his holy presence. The LORD maintained his fellowship with them only by giving them prophets to speak his words to them and priests to make sin offerings for them. The LORD and his people fellowshipped in the Temple. They in the courts, he in the Holy of Holies, together yet separate.

But when the Word became flesh, the barrier came down. He who had been separate from his people in the Holy of Holies, now brushed arms with them in a lowly tabernacle of flesh. He did this so that he, himself, could work our salvation. As a man, he perfectly fulfilled the Law. Then as high priest, he presented his perfect life as an atoning sacrifice for our sins. Only God's Word could fulfil this mission. For he alone possessed the infinite love and righteousness required.

A lifetime of gratitude should be our response to so great a sacrifice made on our behalf.

DECEMBER 18

A God Who Speaks

He committed no sin, and no deceit was found in his mouth (1 Peter 2:22).

Of every person's heart but one can it be said, 'The heart is deceitful above all things and beyond cure' (Jeremiah 17:9). And every man's tongue but one overflows with ungodly speech from the fullness of his contaminated heart. Jesus is that one exception. As Son of man and Son of God, his human heart was filled with godly purity. And that purity overflowed as godly speech.

Jesus used words perfectly. With them he built up his disciples by encouraging and correcting them according to their needs. With them, he prayed to his Father, in intercession and thanksgiving. And with them, he returned his enemies' insults not with threats or retaliation, but with forgiveness.

Jesus' life is our model of a godly tongue; but his death is the cure for our ungodly tongues. His death brought the needed cleansing for our hearts and made the way for the Spirit's renewal of all aspects of our lives, even our speech. He will continue working in us until the day when Zephaniah's words about us are fulfilled: 'They will speak no lies, nor will deceit be found in their mouths.'

DECEMBER 19

Jesus: God's Authority In Flesh

The people were amazed at his teaching, because he taught them as one who had authority... (Mark 1:22).

'Thus saith the LORD' was the preamble to every prophet's speech. And 'One rabbi's opinion is...' was how the teachers of the law discussed the Law. A prophet was only a messenger for God and a teacher of the law was only an interpreter of his words. These men knew their words were significant only because they rested on the authority of God's words.

No wonder the crowds were amazed at Jesus' teaching! For the usual acknowledgements of prophet and teacher were conspicuously missing. His discourses began with 'I tell you the truth', and were filled with references to his own authority: '...if anyone keeps my word, he will never see death' (John 8:51). Previously there was only his written word to give us understanding. Now, with Jesus, God has given us his word in flesh, 'so that we may know him who is true' (I John 5:20).

Lord, make us better stewards of the gospel accounts so that through deeper study we can know you better.

DECEMBER 20

The Long Wait

To us a Son is given
(Isaiah 9:6).

Expectant parents have only months to anticipate their child's arrival. But here was a child whose coming was foretold thousand of years in advance. Even in Eden when death's curse was fresh, he was mentioned as Adam's seed who would bruise the head of that serpent, Satan. Thousands of years ahead, Abraham was promised that his offspring would bless all the nations; and David, that his son would reign for ever. Prophecies multiplied as the birth date drew within a millennium: he would be born in Bethlehem to a virgin, and would grow up to teach in parables and heal the sick. Though a man, he would be called 'Mighty God, Everlasting Father.' His death would be filled with agony as God's wrath fell upon him in place of others. After his death he would be raised once more to life.

This Son was given to us - to all humanity - to free us from sin's captivity. It would not do to keep secret this child's arrival. For all centuries of humanity have needed to know that the Hope of Life was coming. Let us make sure that none of our acquaintances remain unaware of his arrival.

DECEMBER 21

Joseph, A Righteous Man

Joseph her husband was a righteous man and did not want to expose [Mary] to public disgrace (Matthew 1:19).

Here is one of the few glimpses we have of Joseph, Jesus' foster-father. Matthew tells us that Mary and Joseph were legally bound to be married, but 'before they came together, she was found to be with child.' We don't know if he allowed her an explanation. But who would believe such a story? Joseph assumed it was another man.

Joseph, a law-abiding person, would divorce Mary as the law required. Most people, given the situation, would have enjoyed heaping upon the offender the disgrace that a public divorce trial would bring. No doubt Joseph felt hurt, angry and disgraced. But his righteousness prohibited him from using the law to lash out at Mary. His was the righteousness of God: justice mingled with goodness, kindness and mercy. He could not avoid what was right - a divorce - but he would shield Mary from further disgrace by filing it privately.

When an angel explained the truth in a dream, Joseph forgot the divorce. But we should not forget Joseph's righteousness. When we are wronged we should remember kindness, mercy and goodness, as well as justice.

DECEMBER 22

Mary, A Remarkable Woman

The angel went to [Mary] and said, 'Greetings, you who are highly favoured! The Lord is with you.' (Luke 1:28).

Mary was, indeed, highly favoured by God. Through her would come the One on whom all history pivoted. Scripture does not disclose any extraordinary trait in Mary that would have merited God's special favour. But it does reveal her as a woman of remarkable faith and humility - two traits that mark God's most eminent servants.

Mary had great faith to believe God's plan. The incarnation is still a difficult concept today, even after centuries of study. How much greater faith did Mary have to believe that God could have a Son in flesh, when in her day that idea would be unthinkable blasphemy?

Mary's faith enabled her to believe a plan she could not comprehend, but her humility enabled her joyfully to submit to it. Even though a virgin pregnancy would bring her misunderstanding and hardship, she humbly responded, 'I am the Lord's servant. May it be to me as you have said.'

May God make us full of his 'ordinary' traits of faith and humility like Mary so that our lives might bear the marks of God's greatest servants, as hers did.

DECEMBER 23

News For All

> I bring you good news of great joy that will be for all the people (Luke 2:10).

The first impulse of parents after their child's birth is to announce its arrival. And upon Jesus' birth, God immediately set about proclaiming his Son's arrival. This was a royal birth: the Son of the Most High had come. One might expect that only the highest society would view this baby. Yet the only known visitors received that night were the lowliest sort. It was shepherds who heard the angel's glorious bidding: 'Go to Bethlehem and see this thing that has happened.'

Why they were chosen of all those who were crowded into Bethlehem is unknown. Perhaps he chose shepherds, reputed to be poor and far from respectable, because they epitomised those he had come to save. This Saviour was 'for all the people' and no person who came to him for salvation, regardless of station or reputation, would he turn away. So the shepherds went and adored: they departed and rejoiced, spreading the news as they went.

We, too, may go and adore, depart and rejoice in our Saviour. For he esteems none of us too lowly to be received. His salvation is great enough even for our sin.

DECEMBER 24

A Brilliant Message

I will also make you a light for the Gentiles, that you may bring my salvation to the ends of the earth (Isaiah 49:6).

Astrology dominated the lands east of Judah. And the Magi, as the foremost astrologers, were commended for their ability to foretell future events by the stars. Stars, they believed, rose with people. Bright ones for the rich and powerful; small, dim ones for the weak.

But the LORD detested astrology. In Israel, its practice was punishable by death. Stars were for gazing at, not for fortune-telling. They were to seek the LORD for any information they needed.

So, how extraordinary it is that the LORD actually gave the Magi a brilliant star to announce his Son's birth. The LORD wanted to bring these Gentiles to his True Light, so he gave them a sign they could understand. It was as clear as handwriting. They saw the star and journeyed to find the King it represented.

The star of Bethlehem is a sign to us, also. It reminds us that there is always hope for unconverted loved ones. Our God is willing to use even the most unlikely means to bring his message to those who yet don't know him.

DECEMBER 25

The Finest Gifts

[The Magi] saw the child ... and they bowed down and worshipped him (Matthew 2:11).

The most obvious gifts given to the Christ Child were the Magi's gold, frankincense and myrrh; but they were not the only ones. Both Magi and shepherds gave Jesus two more important gifts: the gifts of sacrifice and worship.

Both Magi and shepherds willingly left behind their livelihood to seek the Saviour. For the Magi this meant an arduous, expensive, even dangerous, journey towards an unknown western destination. For the shepherds, this meant leaving their flocks unattended or in the care of others. This was risky either way. For wolves took unattended sheep as an opportunity for dinner; and shepherds, infamous for thieving, could find sheep-sitting an opportunity for sheep-snatching.

Then, as each found the Child, they gave him the gift of worship in faith. The Magi bowed to Jesus, the great King of the Star. The shepherds worshipped him as Saviour. Both worshipped him in faith. For only in faith could anyone bow at the feet of a helpless child of poor parents and believe him a great king. These men gave the best gifts that can ever be given to Jesus, then and now.

DECEMBER 26

A Puzzling Storeroom

But Mary treasured up all these things and pondered
them in her heart (Luke 2:19).

Mary's response to the shepherd's angel story was not
amazement, but awe. The events of the past nine
months had made news of this sort very believable.
She simply placed their story in her heart along with
the others. When she gazed around her heart's storeroom, it was no surprise that what she saw made her
ponder. For there was such a sharp contrast in events.
This Son of God Most High was laid in a feeding-
trough and welcomed by lowly shepherds. Surely he
who wrought a virgin birth didn't lack the power to
make room reservations and prepare a royal welcom-
ing party! These puzzling contrasts seemed inten-
tional, and her mind strove to grasp their meaning.

As he grew up and began his ministry, Mary must
have noticed that the contrasts continued. He, the
Word of God, scorned by the teachers of the law? He,
the one who did no wrong, put to death on a cross?
Only after his resurrection could she harmonise who
he was with how he was treated. All the events of his
life, starting with his birth, were suited to his mission,
not to his glory.

DECEMBER 27

The Light Of The World

> This child is destined to cause the falling and rising of many in Israel ... so that the thoughts of many hearts will be revealed (Luke 2:34-35).

Jesus' birth had been an occasion for rejoicing. At last the Bright Morning Star was sending his rays of truth, righteousness and mercy into the dark land of men. His light would unite Gentile and Jew. God's salvation now extended to all nations. But as Simeon prophesied, it would also divide. A great spiritual struggle would result as the Light exposed the hearts of all. Many would 'rise' as they came to the light to be exposed and cleansed. Many would 'fall' as they hid themselves to prevent exposure. No longer would it be nation against nation. Now it would be 'father against son, and son against father' (Luke 12:53) as each made his own response to the Light.

Jesus' words are as divisive now as then. We all sorrow to see loved ones make an opposing decision. But although we cannot change a person's decision for them, there are things we can do: we can shed the light of a faithful witness and diligently pray for the Holy Spirit to enlighten their hearts.

DECEMBER 28

The Divine Appointment

Prepare to meet your God, O Israel (Amos 4:12).

In Moses' time, the LORD first met with the Israelites to offer them his covenant of eternal love and faithfulness. And although they accepted its terms, they quickly disobeyed them. After hundreds of years of unheeded discipline, the LORD sent word that Israel should prepare to meet him again - this time to receive the fruits of their disobedience. When Jesus came the first time, he brought the new covenant. It extended to all nations, not just Israel. Those who received it would become children of God. Heaven would be their home.

But in the hundreds of years since the covenant was offered, relatively few have accepted it. God mercifully waits. He is not wanting that anyone should perish (2 Peter 3:9). But the day is coming when he will come again. And those who have refused the offer will have to prepare to meet him once more. But having left off meeting him as Friend and Saviour, they must now prepare to meet him as Judge. These are sobering thoughts for all. Let us make sure of our acceptance of his offer as 'Saviour' so that we may not have to face him as Judge.

DECEMBER 29

Who Is The Fool?

Be very careful, then, how you live - not as unwise, but as wise, making the most of every opportunity, because the days are evil (Ephesians 5:15-16).

The wise and the foolish are not categorised by how much knowledge they possess so much as by their use of what they possess. Many know the gospel, yet reject it. They are the fools of Jesus' First Coming. But those who have accepted Jesus' message, the wise of his first coming, must be careful not to become the fools of his Second Coming. For we know that Jesus is returning and that this world is passing away. And our lives should bear fruit from this knowledge.

If we are to be the wise of the Second Coming, we need to follow Paul's exhortation to squeeze from each day all the good it can give. We should live each day with the Great Day before us, to help us steer clear of evil and to encourage us as to the temporary nature of any hardships we face.

At this year's end, let us consider the foolishness we have committed. And ask God for forgiveness and help to make more of the opportunities he gives us in the New Year.

DECEMBER 30

The Great Unknown

No eye has seen, no ear has heard, no mind has conceived what God has prepared for those who love him... (1 Corinthians 2:9).

It is the believer's joy that God has so ordered things as to make these words true for the entire length of their existence. It is true for their time on earth. Others may worry about what is yet unseen, unheard and unconceived, but believers have answered the First Advent's invitation and have become children of God. So their hearts are filled with his promises that the future holds for them only what he has prepared for them. Whatever lies ahead will eventually work for their good.

And though they have these great assurances for their earthly existence, it is with the Second Advent that their joy comes to full blossom. For he who has been Friend and Saviour, will then become Bridegroom. And he will usher into Paradise those who love him, to be his Bride. We cannot overestimate the joy it will be. Free from sadness and pain. Free from being people who do what they should not do, and do not do what they should. Free to know him as he has known us. So we cry, 'Come, Lord Jesus, Come!'

DECEMBER 31